THE SORRENTO EXPERIENCE

by

Gordon Longworth

Checked and approved by the Tourist Office

INTRODUCTION

This guide tells you all you need to know about holidaying in Sorrento, and so much more. Reading it before you go will give you a flavour of the place, an introduction to the treats in store, and help in planning the best use of your time there.

You will meet the people and their way of life: on foot, in cars, and everywhere on their beloved scooters. There is information on where to go, what to do and where to stay. From where to find toilets and banks, to once-in-a-lifetime stuff like how to get married in Sorrento. It's all here.

You don't want to spend your precious holiday time finding mundane stuff for yourself. With so much to see and do you need a guide. The Sorrento Experience aims to tell you all you need to know.

Author Gordon Longworth writes... In the course of many visits, Sorrento became like a second home to me and my family. In the absence of a decent guide, I made my own notes, published as an eBook in 2008. I created an updated edition with double the content in 2013 and included experiences as well as facts. Continued feedback from visitors, augmented by time spent around the town, sitting at cafes and bars, soaking up the ambience and wondering how Italians manage to look so stylish no matter what they are wearing, persuaded me that it was time for another update, and here it is, fresh for summer 2016.

I have provided links to web pages so you can get more detail if you require it, and for information that could be subject to change.

Comments from readers:

"We are just back from Sorrento after a really enjoyable visit and what a great asset your guide was!" – Yana P

"The weather is great and we were laughing about your description of trying to cross the roads here. Great stuff. We're set for a fantastic week and will make very good use of the guide. Thanks again." – Les & Eileen S

"We absolutely love the guide so far, and can't wait to use it! It is full of very useful facts which we will be using. The guide will be great by giving us the do's and don'ts." – Gareth E

"I quickly read the first few pages and after picking myself off the floor with laughing, thought I would email you. This is the way guides should be written. Once again thanks for a great guide." – Derek B

Gordon Longworth

July 2016

ACKNOWLEDGEMENTS

Once I had decided to write a guide, I was fortunate enough to meet Marina O'Keeffe. She was then managing the Citalia office in Sorrento. She gave up a lot of her time answering my questions both at the time and in subsequent correspondence. When I last met her she was the Area Controller for Citalia and still happy to answer questions. This guide might never have got under way without Marina's help.

My enthusiasm for the guide was dampened by the reactions of many publishers, all of them blind to statistics of the number of visitors to Sorrento. Then self-publishing became a reality and reawakened my interest, so I chose a visit in summer 2007 to complete my research.

Help came from Vanessa. She was a tour guide with Goldentours. In the course of a day's trip to Amalfi and Ravello, she taught everyone a little Italian, recounted many anecdotes, brought the experience to life with her commentary and facts, and had a lovely sense of humour. She cajoled her driver into patience at the scenic points or when confronted by impossible traffic situations *"Piano, piano"* (slowly, slowly). She talked incessantly in perfect English all the way from Sorrento to Amalfi. After lunch I met her again in Ravello. She filled in many blanks.

Towards the end of my stay I made an appointment with the Tourist Office. There it was my pleasure to meet Fabiola Fasulo. She was the embodiment of everything Italian. She patiently answered my queries with the elegant hand gestures that the Italians do so well. Since then she has read every draft and painstakingly provided the corrections, updates and advice to make this a guide that is endorsed by the Tourist Office.

From the internet world my thanks go to Chris Payne. Chris is the perfect example of reincarnation. I believe he's been around before as Hawkeye, Attila the Hun and Mahatma Gandhi. His eye for detail picked up so many improvements, his responses fired back at me so quickly they played havoc with my procrastination skills, and whenever I thought I could relax a little, he fired me up again. Thanks Chris. You got me there in the end.

I'm grateful to so many other people who have added to my own experiences. Most of them are nameless - travel reps, tour guides, receptionists, waiters, bar staff, shopkeepers, travellers - the list goes on.

Finally, a great big thank you to all the Italians in and around Sorrento whose spontaneity, style, and music have made all of my visits there so memorable. I take "Come Back to Sorrento" as a personal invitation.

TABLE OF CONTENTS

PART 1 - WELCOME

ABOUT SORRENTO

Sorrento is a city. Being a city conjures up images of something that Sorrento is not. It's not big. It's not industrial. It feels more like a town, and that is the way I tend to write about it. What it is, is a resort, endlessly fascinating in itself, and also providing a base for many other places that really should be on your list of places you must see before you die. If you want preview of Heaven, this is probably as close as you can get.

Sorrento is set on a cliff top 160 feet above the sea, amid some of the most beautiful scenery you are likely to find anywhere in the world. Its resident population of 18,000 is swollen to many times that number in the holiday season.

It's easy to get around on foot as the town itself is basically quite flat. One of the two ports requires some effort, but there is regular public transport to both of them.

Sorrento has its share of high quality shops, but the fascination for me is to wander around the narrow streets and piazzas, lined with little shops, cafes, bars and ice cream parlours, to a background of Neapolitan music. Forget the busy, busy of your workaday life, sit back with a drink or an ice cream, soak up the sun and watch the world go by.

I've always felt safe in Sorrento - no drunkenness, no visible crime, no yobbish behaviour, no apparent threats.

In many visits I have never found any cause for concern.

THE HISTORY BIT

Sorrento is from the Latin *Surrentum*, or *Surriento* in the Neapolitan dialect. It is in the south of Italy in the province of Naples, on the west coast of the region of *Campania*. This is also known as *Campania Felix* - the happy land.

The origins of Sorrento are hidden in the mists of time and entwined with mythology. Sorrento is thought to have been around since pre 474 BC. The name is believed to come from the myths of mermaids who tried to lure Ulysses (Odysseus in Greek mythology) from his mission. They failed. He was made of sterner stuff, being Greek. Although Ulysses continued on his way, it is thought that other Greeks were the first people to settle here. Evidence of this includes the *Marina Grande Gate*, which you will pass through on the way to *Marina Grande*.

Roman involvement in its development is apparent in the design of the old part of the town, known unromantically as "The Drains". This is the street layout of straight roads crossed at right angles by other straight roads. I can never bring myself to call it the Drains. To me it's the Old Town, and that's what I call it throughout this guide.

Over the years the area has seen many cultural influences - Samnite, Roman, Byzantine, Bourbon, French, Spanish, invasion by Turks, and now invasion by tourists.

AIRPORT ARRRIVALS

At The Airport

The airport is Naples *Capodichino*. There is a coin in the slot charge of €1 for trolleys.

Toilets are clean and free.

If your luggage has not arrived, contact the airline representative, who will complete a Property Irregularity Report and give you a copy. Don't leave the airport without it. Request cash for emergency expenditure. You may be out of luck, but at least try.

There is a free, unlimited, internet connection in all airport areas accessible by Wi-Fi. Access it by connecting to the Gesac network. Then register on the welcome page or directly through your Facebook, Twitter or LinkedIn account.

There are Travelex offices in both the arrivals (08.00-23.30) and departures (05.30-22.00) areas.

The Journey

Transfers to Sorrento are best by road. Don't even think about the other options of railway or ferry unless you are backpacking. Not even then. As a stranger you really don't want to be wandering around Naples if you don't know the way.

By Road

It's 49km from Naples to Sorrento. Journey time is about 80 minutes from airport to resort.

If you are relying on public transport, buses go from the airport Arrivals area to Sorrento. They arrive in Sorrento at the *Circumvesuviana* train station, and depart from there if you are returning to the airport that way.

They are run by *Curreri Viaggi*. Fare is €10.00. Get your ticket from the airport newsstand or on board the bus.

Stops along the way are at PompeiScavi, Castellammare, Vico Equense, Meta, Piano, and S.Agnello

The timetable from the airport to Sorrento as I write this (April 2016) is:

09.00

11.00

12.00

13.00

14.30

16.30

18.00

19.30

And from Sorrento Circumvesuviana railway station to the airport at:

06.30

08.30

09.00

10.30

12.00

14.00

15.00

16.30

The timetable changes according to season. You can get the current times from the Tourist Office website at:

http://www.sorrentotourism.com/_downloads/4052-Italiano-curreri-1542016-15112016.pdf

On the way you will pass Vesuvius and the towns it buried in AD79 - Pompeii, Herculaneum, and Stabia. Vesuvius is on the left. The sea is on the right hand side of the road and provides the best views on your journey.

The full name of Stabia now is Castellammare di Stabia (Castellammare, formerly Stabia. *Castellammare* means castle on the sea.) The castle is pretty modest as castles go. There are shipyards here, and it's well known for its thermal waters. It's also the family home town of Al Capone. You can take a cable car from the *Circumvesuviana* station up *Monte Faito*.

On your left you are passing the *Monti Lattari* (the Milky Mountains, so called because they are limestone, and also because that's where the cows live who provide the milk for Mozzarella cheese, which you will find served everywhere in the area).

After Castellammare, and just before Vico Equense, comes Bikini Beach. You get the first views to Sorrento on the right, across the Bay of Naples, and impressive it is, too. You can also see the plastic palm tree that is sited in the bay just off the coast each year. The pizza in its present form originated in Vico Equense, being made at the request of Queen Margherita. The original was made with tomatoes, Mozarella cheese, and basil to represent the colours of the Italian flag of red, white and green.

Vico Equense is the first of the five communities of Sorrento and is 15km from Sorrento itself. This is where the main road, the *Corso Italia*, starts. It passes through the other communities of Meta, Piano di Sorrento, Sant'Agnello (about 1km away), and then Sorrento itself.

By Train and Boat

If this is your choice, you first need to go to Naples. That's about 7km from the airport.

BUSES TO NAPLES

Alibus runs from the airport to both the Central Train Station (*NapoliCentrale*) and to the *Molo Beverello Port* (*Piazza Municipio*). These are the only two stops. The service runs from 6a.m. to midnight at 20 minute intervals (30 minutes at weekend) and takes 25-30 minutes. You can get tickets at Sun Store in the passenger area. You can also pay on the bus at a slightly higher cost.

Train

The train from Naples is the *Circumvesuviana*, downstairs from the main station in *Piazza Garibaldi*. Journey time is about one hour and costs €3.60.

Boats

Sail from *Molo Beverello* at *Piazza Municipio*. This is opposite the *Castel Nuovo*. Sorrento is across the Bay. Journey time on the jetfoil is 35 minutes.

Taxi

The taxi rank is outside the Arrivals area. Official taxis are white and are marked *Comune di Napoli*. Only ever use these in and around Naples. They will take you to the station or ferry. They have a meter and a card showing flat rates to various destinations.

Taxis to Sorrento can be pre-booked and will set you back €90.00 and upwards, depending on the time of year and the amount of luxury you want.

Car Hire

There are desks in the Arrivals hall for Alamo, Avis, Budget, Europcar, Hertz, Maggiore, National, Sixt, and Auto Europa.

Driving in Naples is only for the brave or the foolhardy. If you want a car for your holiday, then go to your accommodation by one of the alternative ways, and hire a car when you get to your destination.

Bear in mind that what you need to drive around here are

suicidal tendencies, tranquillisers and divine help.

Private Arrangements

Most hotels will be able to arrange transport from the airport. These can be booked directly with the hotel.

MEET THE ITALIANS

The Passeggiata

Night time is a family scene with the *passeggiata*. The main road is closed to traffic and the people stroll up and down, greeting friends, sharing stories and, as ever, looking stylish. Young children, even babies, are out at 11.00pm. The streets get quite crowded, especially at weekends. When do they sleep?

It's never time to say goodnight in Sorrento!

Motorists

The Italians drive like no others. They ignore all laws when in motion, then park where there is no parking space. They seem to have two horns and no brakes, although there did seem to be much less use of the horn on my last visit.

It was early in the first week of my first holiday there that I realised that Italian drivers regarded pedestrians as expendable, crossings as target practice, and one-way streets as a challenge. Parking was innovative. It was difficult to tell whether a car was parked, out of fuel, or the driver had just gone for a chat with someone nearby. A major priority in all this mayhem was learning how to cross the road and live.

Scooters carried as much as estate cars. Here, in Sorrento, I had observed a family of three plus a dog on a scooter. I had seen another scooter apparently driven by a large plant, the driver only becoming visible as he went past, his eyes peering through the foliage.

One hot August afternoon, I sat in the shade in the Piazza San Antonino to watch the world go by. In front of me, parked between two cars, was a scooter. I thought about the freedom it could give. Hiring a scooter next day for a trip to Positano along the Amalfi Drive seemed like an attractive idea.

While I pondered on this, a small Fiat appeared. There wasn't enough room for it to park – a minor detail as it turned out. The driver assessed the situation at a glance and immediately reversed into the space. There was a fearful crunch as he hit the scooter, depositing it on the pavement, leaving one wheel protruding into the road.

A vague smell of petrol hovered in the air. The driver got out, barely glanced at me, hefted the scooter completely onto the pavement, then shunted back and forth to nudge the other cars and make more room for himself. Passers-by paid no attention. This appeared to be routine parking procedure. The driver hurried into a nearby shop.

I waited. I hoped that the owner of the scooter would appear and tear the ears off the Fiat driver. Unfortunately the Fiat was away first. There was a little more mayhem with the surrounding cars as he left, but they were probably well dented already. The scooter lay forlornly where it had been deposited, as though it knew its place in the scheme of things.

Suddenly, driving to Positano lost its appeal. A sea trip seemed more appealing.

Most cars are scraped or dented. This is no exaggeration - check them out. The strange thing is that I've never, ever, seen a moving traffic accident. Just mementoes of parking. I have a theory that cars are supplied with dents from new. Gives them street cred.

For people used to driving on the left i.e. principally those from the UK, when you are a pedestrian standing at the pavement edge waiting to cross, first danger is from traffic coming from the left (except on one-way streets! Actually on one-way street too, as one way seems to be an alien concept.)

Some drivers have taken to stopping at pedestrian crossings. This is quite new in my experience, but unfortunately it's impossible to say who might stop and who will attempt to navigate around you. The general rule seems to be that they will stop rather than actually knock you down, but it's a marginal decision for them, and it takes strong nerves to cross the road. It's best to cross at the same time as small boys, as they learn their roadcraft from being perched on their parents' scooters from an early age. You can see whole families on a single scooter.

One of the interests you can undertake in Sorrento is looking for the most outrageous cargo, human and otherwise, on a scooter. And if you want to see an Italian drool, just watch if a Ferrari goes past.

One day I was chatting to a very pretty English girl called Sharon. She had lived in Sorrento for a couple of years whilst working for one of the tour companies, and she told me the secret of driving in Italy - you have to be born there. She had got used to it by hitting things, and now drives on the pavement and goes the wrong way down one way streets with the best of them. If stopped, she cries and tells the police that someone told her to go that way. Being pretty helps, too.

Pets

The locals in Sorrento don't seem to care all that much for cats and dogs. Those you see around are often strays, and lead a pitiful existence, many in need of a visit to the vet. At one time there was a lady who fed stray cats on a site that was later being renovated. This was on *Via Tasso*, at the end near the Hotel Tramontano. There were many cats there. I used to give her a few lira, as it was then, to help with her costs. She was always grateful, and recognised another cat lover.

On my last visit, the cats were there, but not the lady, and not much evidence of food. Next time I'm in Sorrento I'll buy some hard cat biscuits at the supermarket and carry them around. Maybe you could do that too.

Other places where there are many stray cats are the grounds of the *Circolo dei Forestieri* and at *Marina Grande*.

Festivals

There always seems to be something going on in Sorrento, whether on sea or land.

Valentine's Day is also the feast of *S Antonino* with many activities, special events and music.

At Easter there are two processions. The first is on Good Friday at 3.30am. It represents the Madonna looking for Jesus. The participants are led by a brass band as they walk slowly through the town. They wear white gowns and hoods. Followers carry symbols of the crucifixion. Then in the evening of Good Friday in the second procession, the men wear black robes and hoods. It represents the mourning after Christ's death. I haven't been there at Easter, hence the lack of more personal detail.

However, twice I have been there for the *Festival of Sant' Anna*. This is on the first Sunday after July 26. Festivities actually start on the Thursday before that. If you are around at the time of the festival, don't miss it, although really it would be hard to avoid.

It really came to my attention on the Sunday morning whilst still in bed.

The day started with an almighty bang at 8.00, closely followed by two more explosions loud enough to make your teeth rattle. *Mamma mia!* What was that?

An early call is one thing, but this was going well over the top, even for the Italians.

Never one to start the day by jumping out of bed, I lay there collecting my thoughts for a quarter of an hour, when there was another salvo of three. Clearly there was to be no more sleep. Before 9.00 there had been three more barrages, and a pattern had begun to emerge. Each time a ship pulled away from the Marina Piccola and passed alongside Marina Grande, it sounded its siren three times, and this was answered by the volley of three rockets from the shore.

At breakfast we enquired of the waiter. "Ah, c'e Sant'Anna", he said with a shrug. The patron saint of gunpowder, it seems.

So we had managed to hit the Festival of S Anna. She is the patron saint of Marina Grande. The festivities that had started a few days ago were due to end in the evening with Mass, followed by a parade through the old town.

We decided to check out the progress of the Festival by walking down to Marina Grande.

At the marina, we were not alone. The festivities were in full swing, in a laid back sort of way. A band was playing, perhaps with about 40 enthusiastic members. They assaulted one tune while we listened from a safe distance, then moved further along the waterfront before stopping to give another spirited rendition to those people who had escaped the first. Ten out of ten for effort.

The waterfront was lined with stalls, selling a huge range of goodies. Sweets in all shapes and sizes, every imaginable variety of nut - pistachio, monkey nuts, nuts covered in chocolate, chestnuts, and more. There were many stalls of children's toys of the cheap plastic variety. My son, in his younger days, would have loved it. He once spent most of a week when we were holidaying half way up a mountain in Austria with eyes only for the bubble gum machine outside the hotel.

The procession in the evening is a moving scene. You hear the singing as the procession draws near. First come the children hand in hand with their mums. The last time I saw it, a young teenager wearing a white gown with red trimmings, and somehow incongruously wearing black trainers, carried a pole bearing a pair of loudspeakers surmounted by an aerial, to relay the service and instructions from elsewhere in the procession. Clearly this was a hi-tech event. Elders of the church went past in their regalia - white gowns with blue capes and sashes, and medallions the size of plates.

When the procession came to one of many temporary halts beside where I was standing, one of the crowd stepped forward and grabbed hold of one of these medallions to inspect it more closely. The wearer of the medallion was less than pleased. Gazing upwards he mouthed something which was inaudible from where I stood. I waited for the intruder to be struck by a thunderbolt, but then the procession moved on again and he was spared.

The group carrying the statue of S Anna came into view. This was the statue that, at other times, adorns the *Church of S Anna* in *Marina Grande*. Then, bringing up the rear, were the ordinary folk of the fishermen's port - families following behind the figure of their patron saint. The whole procession was an intensely emotional experience.

We tagged along with the end of the procession to follow the crowd down to the Marina Grande. Progress was slow, but typically good-humoured.

The band was down there again, apparently fully recovered from its efforts earlier in the day, and more than ready to dish out some more of the same to the fairly static crowd that was shuffling slowly past. The band got under way just as we drew alongside. There was no escape in the crowd. The conductor appeared part way through their opening number, bowed to the captive audience to a little sporadic clapping and much indifference. There was no noticeable change in the performance when he started conducting, leading to the opinion that they weren't all playing the same tune anyway, or at least not the same parts of it. They seemed to bring the same carefree anarchy to their music as to their driving.

Moving to a safer distance we sat on a wall beside an Italian family. They had bought some delicacies from one of the stalls, and invited us to share them. The titbits on offer looked like butter beans in brine - lupini as I learned later. Not to my taste, but it was only as I chewed manfully at one, attempting to look duly grateful, that I saw our new friends convulsed at my efforts. The *Mamma* indicated that I should have taken the shell off first. To cement Anglo/Italian relations we gratefully accepted two more, did as the natives did, and ate them without shells. They tasted the same. Must be an acquired taste.

The Festival culminates in an impressive firework display over the harbour. Views from the hotels on the *Via del Capo* are amazing. The fireworks are launched from a boat in the bay. I watched this display once from a balcony at the Hotel Bristol and it seemed to be in the middle of it all. It sets off car alarms and dogs barking. It's not the time for an early night.

The enthusiasm for life is a most engaging feature of Italian temperament during the day, but more difficult to come to terms with when trying to sleep. Italians, of course, never sleep except during the day when you want to buy something.

Girl Appreciation Society

The tarantella is a pretty hectic folk dance. There are different versions of it in different regions. It looks good when done by professional groups. It looks pretty exhausting when done by couples. Our first experience of it was at a bar on the *Corso Italia* on our first night in Sorrento. The bar is no longer there.

We were sitting there enjoying the Neapolitan music when we noticed a smoothly groomed Italian looking our way. He was very noticeable in a sharply cut dark suit, black bow tie, black and white patent spats shoes, hair slicked back. He looked the embodiment of every Mafioso I'd ever imagined or seen on film. I tried not to look his way, but whenever I glanced in his direction he seemed to be watching us. Then he got up and walked towards us. His walk was confident. He looked like someone not to be messed with.

He bowed extravagantly, gleaming white teeth, and indicated that he wanted my wife to dance. My presence was apparently of no consequence. My wife can manage a languid shuffle around the dance floor, but this was announced as a Tarantella. She declined. His teeth flashed some more and he moved smoothly on. He was more successful with the Latin lovely he approached next, and they put on a spectacular show. It seemed to entail much hand clapping and bobbing about, with movements like a cross between a Viennese waltz and a Lancashire clog dance.

We left soon afterwards for the trek back to our hotel in Sant'Agnello. He was still with his tarantella partner, but looked up as we left. I was pleased to wake next morning to find that I was still sharing a bed with my wife and not with a horse's head.

This all happened before I had had time to discover that Sorrento had little crime, and that the typical Italian will take every opportunity to chat up any girl, attached or otherwise.

AROUND TOWN

The Old Town

As I mentioned earlier, this area is called "The Drains", but not by me. It's the part of Sorrento that I love the best.

Narrow streets, paved with the lava from Vesuvius, and lined with shops of every description from the cheapest *salumeria* to classy fashion stores. Bars and restaurants are everywhere. Local residents in the apartments above haul up their supplies in baskets on the ends of ropes. Music is everywhere.

The *Sedil Dominova* on *Via San Cesareo* is a 16th century building that's worth a look. It was originally a meeting place for noblemen and bears their coats of arms. Now it seems to be more in the nature of a working men's club, where they play cards. *Via San Cesareo* is the one immediately facing you as you approach from *Piazza Tasso*.

Streets are always clean. They are cleaned every day. The main roads, too. You will notice this especially if you have a room overlooking a road. It serves as a wakeup call.

The Squares

Piazza Tasso

The main square is named after the poet *Torquato Tasso*. This is the focal point for the evening *passeggiata* where the locals come to see and to be seen. Streets radiate in all directions from *Tasso* - into the old town, down to the port, out west to the hotels that line the coast road, out to the east to Sant'Agnello, Piano di Sorrento, Meta and on to Naples.

In it is a statue by *Gennaro Cali* of the poet Torquato Tasso, 1544-1595. His most famous poem was *La Gerusalemme Liberata* (Jerusalem Delivered). Be honest - you've never heard of it or him. Well now you can tell people that it was an epic poem about the First Crusade. He went slightly nutty for a time, but was due to be crowned in 1595 as Italy's Poet Laureate when he died.

There is also a statue of Saint Antonino who was a Benedictine monk and is the patron saint of the town. He died in AD830.

Piazza Angelina Lauro

A big, mostly pedestrianised square with palms trees like

gigantic pineapples. Here you can sit at the pavement tables with an ice cream or something more potent. There are two banks, and the main post office is just around the corner.

The tour buses leave from the *Lauro Parking Area* here. This is at the back of the piazza, with access from *Via Correale.*

The road up to the station is opposite, just across the *Corso.*

Piazza S Antonino

This is an attractive little area. It houses the Town Hall (*Municipio*) and the *Basilica of S Antonino.* You can sit here and watch the Italians parking their various vehicles. Prepare to be amazed!
There is a statue of S Antonino and a restaurant/bar.

From here it's only a couple of minutes to the *Circolo dei Forestieri, Teatro Tasso* for the Sorrento Musical, the Public Gardens, and the way down to *Marina Piccola.*

The Ports

There are two ports. You can take an *EAV (Ente Autonomo Volturno)* bus to both of them, but it's no great distance on foot from *Piazza Tasso*. There is no sea level footpath between the two.

Marina Piccola

Piccola means small so, in true Italian style, *Marina*

Piccola is the big one. It's where the cruise ships come in, and where you get ferries to take you to Capri, Naples, Ischia, Positano and Amalfi.

There are four ways to *Marina Piccola* on foot. The first three are all different ways onto the *Via de Maio*. They are:

From *Piazza Tasso* take the steps down. There are 130 steps to the road, the *Via De Maio*. It's then about a five minute straight walk down to the port. The steps down are not a problem, but coming back up them will test your fitness. But you can always get the bus back.

From *Piazza San Antonino*. Walking down from *Piazza Tasso*, turn right at *Piazza San Antonino* and follow the steps down. When you reach the road (*Via De Maio* again) turn left to the next set of steps down in about 30 metres. This will cut out one of the bends in the road. At the bottom turn left down to the port. If you are walking back up from the port, this is a less exhausting route than the straight climb of the 130 steps to *Piazza Tasso*.

Also just after *Piazza San Antonino*. Turn right onto *Via de Maio*. This is the route followed by the bus. It passes the *Circolo Dei Forestieri* and the Tourist Office. It is the only way without steps, and so is theoretically possible for a wheelchair, but because of the road surface, traffic and lack of pavements, it would not be a good idea.

From the *Giardini Pubblici* (Public Gardens). This is a winding slope down except near the bottom where the path enters the cliff face, and there are six very broad steps in the semi-dark. At the bottom are the private beaches, but turn right and follow the path to the port, passing the one stretch of public beach on the way. This is much the easiest way up and down to the port on foot.

There is a lift in the Public Gardens down to the bathing beaches and the port. The fare is €1.00 single, €1.80 return. The fare is collected at the bottom. Although the walk down is easy enough, taking the lift back up can be a life saver on a hot day. It operates from:

October - April	7.30am – 07.30pm
May - September	7.30am – 08.30pm
June - July - August	7.30am -01.00am

Marina Grande

This is, of course, the smaller of the two. It's the fishermen's port. You can see the boats come in here and watch catches of swordfish being unloaded, nets being mended, and cats scavenging for food. But there's more to *Marina Grande* than that. There are some good seafront restaurants. There's a tiny bit of public beach as well as the beaches where you have to pay for admission. It's a place that is well worth a visit. It's quieter than the rest of the town, and more picturesque. You can get here by *EAV* bus or by two roads.

The road along the harbour front is lined with shops and snack bars where the food is very reasonably priced. The shops sell souvenirs, clothes, household linens, refreshments, and toys for the kiddies.

There are dozens of boats of all shapes and sizes bobbing about on the water. There is the odd classy launch, but this is predominantly the fishermen's port.

Most of the locals are in a state of great inactivity, if you can call Italians inactive when they are talking to each other. Certainly they are animated conversationalists. I have a theory that if you tied an Italian's hands behind his back, he would be totally unable to talk.

To get there from *Piazza Tasso*, turn right down *Via San Francesco*. At the end turn left on *Via V Veneto*, passing the Public Gardens and the Imperial Hotel Tramontano. (The house in which *Torquato Tasso* was born is now part of the Tramontano.) Then continue around the *Grande Piazza della Vittoria* (Victory Square).

You are now on the *Via Marina Grande*. At the corner of the *Piazza della Vittoria*, on the cliff top, stands the Bellevue Syrene. The hotel entrance, garlanded with flowers, and backed by the blue of the sea and the sky, is among the most beautiful in Sorrento.

Just beyond the Bellevue the road narrows to little more than a car's width. Don't for a moment think that this will cause cars to slow down. You have to wonder why it is so many years since the Italians had a Formula One world motor racing champion. (Alberto Ascari in a Ferrari in 1953.) Maybe it's because racing cars don't have horns.

Pass the Hotel Regina on the left. This road continues to the port. Nearing the end of the road and just before the way down to the harbour, a shrine to S Anna is built into the wall. Its flaking paintwork and crumbling plaster mirrors that of the houses, but the permanent presence of newly cut flowers shows the reverence that Italians feel for these wayside testaments to their faith. It is illuminated at night.

Then there is a series of broad steps (wide but not steep) that take you down towards the Marina Grande Gate (*Porta della Marina Grande*). This is an old Greek structure dating from the end of the fifteenth century, and was the only way into the town from the sea. Emerge from this and the port comes into view.

There are two more shrines at the top of the last flight leading down to the harbour. They are set high in the wall and surrounded by bougainvillea.

Another way down is from the west end of the *Corso Italia*. Pass the hospital and turn right on the *Via Del Mare*. This is the bus route, and takes you directly to the Marina, but the road doesn't have anything scenic to offer the pedestrian, apart from the ever present adrenalin-pumping thrill of avoiding being knocked down. Part of the way along, the road goes through a tunnel. It's a circuitous route anyway. Much better to go the other way.

A slight alternative to walking the full length of this road is to continue out of town on the main road, the *Corso Italia* becoming the *Via del Capo*. A little way along here, on the right hand side, is the *Nube d'argento International* camping site. You can walk through here and on the edge of the site is a way down to *Via del Mare*.

Beaches

If a beach means sand to you, then there's not too much of it in Sorrento. Most of the beaches are privately owned, with basic entrance being around €10.00. There is one small stretch of public beach at each of the Marinas. Being both small and popular, they get a bit crowded.

The free beach area near Marina Piccola is just a few metres past Peter's Beach. It has been completely renovated and includes toilets and changing room.

Gardens

Public Gardens (*Giardini Pubblici*)

From *Piazza Tasso* at the start of the old town turn right down *Via S Francesco*, continue through *Piazza S Antonino* and the gardens are at the end. Near the entrance is a statue of *S. Francesco*, opposite the Church and *Cloisters of S. Francesco*. The cliff top views are of *Marina Piccola*, the private and public beaches and Vesuvius across the bay. Also this gives access to the easiest way down to the Marina.

It's a pleasant and quiet area. Following the path to the right takes you to a tranquil square where there is usually a spare seat or two.

It's about a five minute walk from *Tasso*, if you don't get diverted by any of the shops en route.

Piazza della Vittoria

Another five minutes from the *Giardini Pubblici,* past the Tramontano, takes you to the *Piazza della Vittoria*. It contains the war memorial and is a pleasant green area. The wall of the Hotel Tramontano is at one end. The front of the Hotel Continental opens on to it, and the Bellevue Syrene is just in front.

By day the square is a haven of peace and quiet, and popular with Italian couples.

It's a nice place for wedding photos, so you may find a little of that taking place.

L'agruminato

This is a public park containing many lemon and orange trees. Access is from *Corso Italia*, just past *Piazza Lauro* and the Post Office, more or less opposite the Hotel Michelangelo.

Churches

There are many churches in Sorrento. Some are so unimpressive from the outside that you might pass them by. Those below are ones that I have been in, and been duly impressed. They are quite breathtaking inside.

Dress appropriately

Italy is a Catholic country. Respect their traditions. If you want to go into a church, please don't wear shorts or miniskirts. Ladies are expected to cover their shoulders and arms, so no off the shoulder clothes. A scarf can be draped over the shoulders. If you don't dress appropriately you will cause offence. If you take a trip to Rome, make sure you take suitable clothes if you wish to visit St Peter's, or you won't be allowed in.

Photography

The insides of these churches are amazing. The paintings on walls and ceilings are superb. Here's a photographic tip. If you want to take photos of ceilings, use the delay setting on your camera, if it has one. Set the delay option, put the camera on the floor of the church, press the shutter release, and move far enough away so that you don't appear in the photo as well. This is where digital scores over film. You can view the results and decide whether you need to do it again with the camera in a slightly different position.

The Cathedral (Duomo)

The Cathedral is on the *Corso Italia*. The bell tower stands separate from the main building. There is an English Mass in the Cathedral at 5pm every Sunday in summer time only (June - September).

The Basilica of S Antonino

The Basilica of S Antonino is in Piazza S Antonino where you will find his tomb. He lived in the sixth century. The walls of the crypt are covered with offerings from the people who have been cured after praying to him - silver hearts, silver lungs, feet, etc.

When last I visited, I passed the priest at the top of the stairs.*"Buon giorno!"* I said, and he greeted me the same way. Twenty minutes or so later I went back up and found that the gates were locked. He had seen me go down. He knew where I was. I wondered what sort of piece of silver would be appropriate if the Saint heard my prayers. I must have made the right invocation because the priest reappeared from somewhere and let me out without a word. I said a quick thank you to S Antonino.

The Church of S Francesco

The church is at the entrance to the public gardens (*Giardini Pubblici*). It has cloisters (*Chiostro di San Francesco*) which are used for concerts and to provide a superb location for weddings. This is where state (i.e. non-religious) weddings are held.

The Church of S Anna

This church is at *Marina Grande*. S Anna is the patron saint of the Marina and of fishermen.

Museums

The Museo Correale di Terranova is in Sorrento. It's on the *Via Correale, 50* which starts at *Piazza Tasso*. The museum is a little way along here, past *Piazza Lauro*. Entrance is €8.00. Summer hours from April 1 2016 to 31 October 2016 are:

Tuesday to Saturday : 9:30 to 18:30

Sunday and holidays : 9:30 to 13:30

Monday : closed

There's a website that can give you a preview:

http://www.museocorreale.it

It's in Italian, but you can translate it or just look at the photographs of the displays.

The museum has twenty rooms of exhibits. It houses archaeological findings from the area, and a room dedicated to Torquato Tasso. These are on the ground floor.

The first and second floors contain 17th and 18th century

paintings, and 18th century furniture, porcelain and Venetian glass

The orange grove in the gardens leads to a belvedere with views over the Bay.

Another museum worth a visit in Sorrento contains beautiful examples of inlaid wood. This is the *Museo Bottega della Tarsia Lignea*. It is closed on Mondays and some public holidays. From 1st April to 31st October it's open from 9.30 to 1.00 and from 4.00 to 8.00. From 1st November to 31st March the times will be 9.30 to 1.00 and 3.00 to 7.00. You can find it at *Via S Nicola, 28.* Admission is €8.00. Its website is:

www.museomuta.it

The *George Vallet Archaeological Museum* is in Piano di Sorrento, in the *Villa Fondi* on the *Via Ripa di Cassano*. For information on the George Vallet Museum you can visit

http://www.sorrentotourism.com/en/museo-georges-vallet.php

It's temporarily closed in April 2016

I think the *EAV* bus to Piano di Sorrento goes along this road on its way either to or from the *Marina di Cassano*, but I can't be sure so you would need to check. The railway station at Piano di Sorrento is the stop after Sant' Agnello. You can walk from there. I guess it would take about ten minutes.

Railway Station

The station is opposite *Piazza Lauro*. This is the

Circumvesuviana, with trains travelling between Sorrento and Naples. It's not main line - the main line station is in Naples.

There is a bust of Giovanbattista De Curtis at the approach to the station. Together with his son Ernesto, he wrote *Torna a Surriento* (Come Back to Sorrento). As a preview of treats in store, you can listen to Pavarotti singing it at:

https://www.youtube.com/watch?v=wbdM7yuNGYI&no html5=False

Cemetery (Cimitero)

This may be a curious thing to have in a guide book, but I love the cemetery.

The cemetery is close to the market. If you go to the market you could look in here at the same time/afterwards/instead of for non-dedicated bargain hunters. After all the frantic activity it's an oasis of calm.

The graves are not a free-for-all. They are of uniform size and style, a bit like the graves in a war cemetery. They often bear a photograph of the deceased, or some memento - a necklace, a child's toys.

After a funeral, flowers not left on the grave are left near the entrance to the cemetery. On my first visit, I was outraged to see a woman helping herself to these. Apparently it is the custom. Instead of being left to be taken away as rubbish, it's preferable to have them taken from there to go on other graves, or to beautify their homes. What a sensible idea.

Because of a lack of space, after a period, I believe it's ten years, bodies are moved from the graves and placed in caskets in the mausoleum or in walls around the grounds.

NEED TO KNOW

Banks

If you want to exchange currencies and travellers cheques, or to buy that villa you've just spotted with views over the bay, there are many banks around in Sorrento:

Banca Popolare di Bari Via degli Aranci, 31

Banca Intesa/Banco Napoli, Corso Italia 210

Banca Della Campania, Corso Italia, 315

Deutsche Bank, Piazza Angelina Lauro, 22 – 27

Banca Sella Sud Spa, Piazza Angelina Lauro, 35

Banca Monte dei Paschi di Siena, Via degli Aranci, 60

Banca Intesa San Paolo IMI, Via San Renato, 2

Banca Nazionale del Lavoro, Via S. Francesco, 5

They are open Monday to Friday. Hours tend to be from about 08.30 to 13.30 and then again from 14.00 to 15.00.

Vehicle rental

There's quite a choice for the rental of cars, scooters and bicycles. For a complete list, see:

http://www.sorrentotourism.com/en/auto-scooter-and-bike-rentals.php

Car Parking

You can view a map of car parks at:

http://www.sorrentotourism.com/ downloads/1968-Italiano-parkingl2014or.pdf

The car park beside *Piazza Lauro* is probably the most central one with access from *Via Correale*. Parking costs €2.00 per hour. Coaches park at ground level. Cars go below.

The one nearest to the port is the Garage Marina Piccola. It's at *Via Luigi De Maio 60/62*. They have a website at:

www.garagesorrento.com/en/

The charge depends on the size of car. Tel +39 081 8781 306.

Electricity

The electric supply is 220v. The plugs have two round pins.

Hospital (Ospedale)

You have to hope you don't need it, but the husband of one lady who spent the last days of her holiday there (and some more as well), said that she was well looked after. I've never used protection against insect bites in Sorrento and have never been bothered by them. She wasn't so lucky.

Standing in *Piazza Tasso*, with your back to the sea, turn right to the hospital. It's about an eight minute stroll, but faster if you are suffering.

If you need an ambulance, dial 118.

Money

Euro banknotes are available as 5, 10, 20, 50, 100, 200, and 500 euros

Euro coins are for 1 or 2 euros

Cents coins are for 1, 2, 5, 10, 20, and 50 cents.

As well as banks and the post office, there are several bureaux de change offices. Those that I have checked charge no commission.

Police

There are three different police departments.

The *Vigili Urbani* are the town hall police. They deal with traffic.

For anything lost or stolen, you need the *Polizia*. If you need to report any problem you must do this within 24 hours of the incident, and take your passport for ID. They also look after safety and traffic control, and general law and order. If you should need them, they are on *Vico III Rota*. This is the third street on the left after *Piazza Lauro* (heading away from *Piazza Tasso*). They wear smart blue uniforms - light blue tops, darker trousers. I've seen them in the tiniest cars, and also on a Segway. (The Segway is a two-wheeled vehicle that you stand on, except for George W Bush, who was filmed falling off one.) It's probably the ideal means of transport around town, taking up little more room than the driver himself. This is a high speed way of catching people who have parked in the wrong place. For the police, call free 113.

More spectacular are the *Carabinieri* with their exquisite uniforms (black, with a red stripe), and imposing presence. From Ray-Bans down to boots they are the epitome of Italian style. A rare breed in Sorrento, their natural habitat is the bigger cities. If you venture to Rome or Naples you are likely to meet some. They are responsible for public order, drugs, crime, and looking impressive. Those in Naples are kept fully occupied by the *Camorra*. The *Carabinieri* are the national police force with military status. They are on *Via Capasso*. This is first on the left after *Piazza Lauro*. Their free number is 112.

Post Office (Ufficio Postale)

The Post Office is on the Corso Italia just round the corner from *Piazza Lauro*. It is open on Monday to Friday from 08.30 to 18.30, and 08.00 to 12.30 on Saturday.

If it's stamps (*francobolli*) you want, they are also sold by *tabacchi*. There are different rates for different countries. Tell them the destination.

Public Toilets

You can find public toilets:

- on the corner of *Piazza Tasso* and *Via Correale*;
- at *Piazza Lauro*;
- in the public gardens (*Villa Comunale*);
- in the free beach area at Marina Piccola
- at the top entrance to the market;
- at Marina Grande, to the right from the bottom of the slope;
- in the building housing the Tourist Office and the Circolo dei Forestieri;

In addition to the public toilets, you can always try the various bars. Some may not be very welcoming, but the Fauno Bar in *Piazza Tasso* has no objections.

Expect to pay 50c at the public toilets. You should leave a similar tip at any bar.

Telephone (Telefono)

You can buy telephone cards (*carte telefoniche*) at the Post Office and *tabacchi*. The usual denominations are €5 or €10. You have to tear off the corner before they become usable. This is marked on the card.

You can use coins (one or two euros).

The cheapest rate for calls is from 22.00 to 08.00 daily, Saturday afternoon, and all day on Sundays and Bank Holidays.

Tipping

Tipping around town for meals and drinks is at discretion, but is usually accepted as being 10% to 15%. If a service charge is included in the bill, it will be shown on the menu as *servizio incluso*. You might still want to leave another 5% if the service warranted it.

For taxis, it's usual to give 10%.

The following guide to tipping in hotels was suggested to me by a holiday rep:

Chambermaid	€5 per room per week
Dining room week	€5 per person per
Porter	€1 per suitcase

Reception	€5 per holiday
Bar	€5 per week

Tourist Information Office

The office is in the grounds of the *Circolo de Forestieri*. The address is: *AAS Azienda Autonoma di Soggiorno Sorrento - Sant'Agnello, Via Luigi De Maio 35 Sorrento*

Tel: +39 081 8074033

Fax: +39 081 8773397

Web: www.sorrentotourism.com

This is an excellent website with masses of useful information. Anything that you can't find in this guide can most likely be found in the website. It's well worth browsing through the site to see what is on offer.

They can provide maps of Sorrento, timetables of local transport, and information about attractions and events. They are English speaking and helpful.

Water

It doesn't kill the Italians, and I've drunk it in small quantities on occasions, but the advice is to use bottled water. The choices are:

Sparkling water is *Acqua minerale con gas*, or *frizzante*

Still water is *Acqua minerale naturale* or *senza gas*

Weather

The most reliable months are April to June. The hottest, driest month is July. August can have just a little more rain.

July and August are the months when most Italians take their holidays, so can be both hot and with more crowds.

Autumn is pleasant, with September being warm, but with a little more chance of rain. October is still pleasantly warm, but has getting on for double the September rainfall. November is the wettest month.

SHOPPING

General

Many shops close for an afternoon siesta which can be from around 1.00pm to around 4.30pm. They are often open to around 10.00pm.

The main products of the area are olive oil (*olio extra vergine d'oliva - DOP* is a registered Italian trademark), inlaid wood (*intarsio*), a lemon liquor (*limoncello*), and cheese (*mozzarella*).

Best buys are cameos, capodimonte, porcelain, inlaid woodwork, leather shoes, belts and bags, table linen (crochet and appliqué) and embroidered goods. Scarves and pashminas are very reasonably priced.

There is nothing much in the way of shops at the two Marinas.

Receipts

Receipts are compulsory and should show the shop name and address, and the Partita IVA (tax code). If you don't ensure that you get a receipt, you could be stopped by the police and fined, so you will need to keep the receipt until you are well clear of the shop or bar where you made your purchase.

The issue of receipts is to stop the shopkeeper from evading payment of tax. As with everything to do with the law in Sorrento, observance tends to be casual, and I don't recall receiving too many receipts. But don't say you weren't told.

Chemists (farmacia)

Chemists are identifiable by a green cross outside. English is usually spoken and, in my experience, the staff are skilled, knowledgeable and helpful. Some medicines requiring prescriptions in the UK do not necessarily require prescriptions here.

Farmacia Farfalla is at *Piazza Tasso, 35.* 08.00-13.30, 15.30-21.00 close to the Excelsior Vittoria

Farmacia Alfani is at *Corso Italia 131*. It's open from 08.30 to 21.00.

Tobacconists/Newsagents (tabacchi)

Tobacconists/newsagents often have a large **T** outside. They sell postcards, stamps, bus tickets and telephone cards.

Foreign newspapers (English, American, French, German) are one or two days old by the time they hit the Sorrento streets.

Supermarkets (Supermercato)

The three main ones are:

Deco

Deco is on the *Corso Italia 221* between *Piazza Tasso* and *Piazza Lauro*.

Weekday hours are 08.30 to 20.30. Sunday 09.00 to 13.00.

Sisa

Sisa is on the corner of *Via degli Aranci* and *Via San Renato*, which is further on from *Piazza Lauro*. It is open 09.00 to 13.30 and 17.00 to 20.55.

Conad

Conad is at *Via Capo 10* which is past the Hospital. It is open 09.00 to 20.00

Clothes

There are clothes for all tastes and wallets. The classier and more pricey ones are on the *Corso Italia*, where you can find Giorgio Armani among others. Venture into the old town and things are cheaper but without the big name labels. The market is cheapest of all.

If you have just won the lottery you can try Capri, where just about every big name is represented. Take a look in the store in Anacapri near to the chairlift. You should be able to find something there to hoover up all your euros. It's worth a visit anyway as it's air conditioned.

Positano also has more than enough boutiques to satisfy the most ardent shopper. Again, the prices may bring tears to your eyes, and to those of your bank manager.

Marquetry (Intarsio)

This is traditional work that goes from generation to generation. Almost 35% of the inhabitants live on making and selling this kind of work. Marquetry is the second largest industry after tourism. Veneers are imported from all over the world. They use mahogany, walnut and rosewood briar. The design is glued down onto a solid piece of mahogany or walnut. It then goes under a press for a couple of days, and is finished with a polyester matt or shiny finish. It won't mark if things are spilled on it, so they say (water, coffee, cigarettes). Small pieces of furniture are packed flat and can be taken. Larger pieces are shipped to anywhere in the world.

There are many workshops and stores around Sorrento. Probably the most famous one is Cuomo's Lucky Store

http://www.cuomosluckystore.it/en/

The name sounds like a cheap bazaar, but don't be fooled. It sells very high class *intarsio* and buyers can make a serious dent in their travel money, albeit with something to treasure forever thereafter. If you want to part with some serious money then come here. It's at *Piazza Antiche Mura*, just up *Via Sersale* by the *Duomo* and through the *Parsano Gate* in the southern wall of the city. It also sells some much cheaper items, and is well worth a visit. They will ship to anywhere in the world. Check that once you are home, if something goes wrong with the piece, you can return it at their expense and you will be sent a replacement completely free of charge.

Beware - cheaper imitations may be using plywood or cheap board instead of solid wood. Even experts cannot always tell the difference. You can only be sure that it is genuine if they issue a written guarantee, registered at the Chamber of Commerce, as Cuomo's does, even for a very small box. They give two guarantees - first that it is genuine inlaid, and second, it is guaranteed against cracking.

Cameos

The first cameos were made in the area around Pompeii.

Cameos are made from sea shells coming from every part of the world. They have three layers. The first layer is removed. The design is carved with little knives out of the second layer, which is white. It is then set in gold or silver. So the colour of the cameo is the colour of the sea shell and the white figure is the second part of the sea shell. Because it's all hand made the value is not based on size or colour - only on the workmanship.

If you buy a cameo, get a certificate to say that it is crafted from a shell. Some could be plastic.

Jewellery

If you've got any money left towards the end of your holiday, and can't bear to take it back home again, there's a shop at *Corso Italia 54* that will be happy to help with your problem. Borriello is a high class jeweller selling watches, gold, coral and cameos. It still brings tears to my eyes when I recall going in there with my wife and coming out with an 18ct gold chain.

In fairness she's had a lot of mileage from it. It comes out regularly, and not just on special occasions.

Music

Traditional Neapolitan music has many characteristics. There is the infectious gaiety of *Oi Mari* and *Funiculi, Funicula*; the romantic sounds of *O Sole Mio* and *Santa*

Lucia. Music is everywhere in Sorrento. It provides a background to your wandering around town, comes over speakers in the old town, and from the bars and cafes at night. To hear Come Back to Sorrento (*Torna a Surriento*) sung in a rich Neapolitan tenor, floating across the still night air from a bar along the Bay, is the ultimate in romance. If you don't fall in love with Sorrento, and more in love with your partner when you hear this, you must have come from another planet.

If you want to take a CD of Italian or Neapolitan music back home with you, try The Jack at *Viale Nizza 17*. This is off the *Corso Italia* on the left, a little way past *Piazza Lauro.*You'll be spoiled for choice. They are happy to play any that you are considering.

Wine etc

You'll find wine stores everywhere in the old town. Take your pick, and don't forget the supermarkets.

You can buy wine at anything from two or three euros upwards. If you are buying wine, you will probably need a corkscrew. If you haven't brought one with you, or a trusty Swiss Army Knife, you'll need to buy one. A corkscrew is a *cavatappi*.

Lacrima Christi (Tear of Christ) is a wine from vineyards on Vesuvius.

Lemon trees are everywhere in and around Sorrento, so it's no surprise to find that a drink is made from them. This is *Limoncello.* You can see it being made as you wander around the old town.

One place you should visit is Vizi & Sfizi at *Via Fuoro 22*. Prepare to be amazed at the selection of drinks available here. You can follow this link for a preview:

http://www.vizisfizi.com/index_12.php

Markets

There's a market in Sorrento on Tuesday mornings from about 08.30 to 13.30. It's off *Via San Renato*. You get to it by following the *Via Marziale*, which goes up past the right hand side of the station. Cross the main road (the *Via degli Aranci*) and continue along *Via Marziale*. Turn right when it joins *Via San Renato*, pass the cemetery on the left, beware all the cars and scooters causing mayhem, and so to the market. It's about a 15 minute walk from *Piazza Tasso*.

There are toilets near the top entrance to the market. They are on the left as you go in from the road.

Also there are markets in Sant'Agnello and Piano di Sorrento every Monday morning.

WHAT'S TO DO?

Go On An Excursion

Many destinations and activities are offered by hotels, by holiday reps and by local tour companies.

Tours provided by Goldentours, with 2016 prices, are:

Amalfi Drive	€38.00
Entrance to Villa Rufolo	*€5.00*
Capri and Anacapri	€78.00
Entrance to Villa S Michelle	*€7.00*
Entrance to Giardini di Augusto	*€1.00*
Pompei and Vesuvio combined	€47.00
Entrance to Pompeii Scavi	*€13.00*
Entrance to Vesuvio	*€10.00*
Pompei and Ercolano	€56.00
Entrance to Pompeii Scavi	*€13.00*
Entrance to Ercolano Scavi	*€11.00*
Rome (one day)	€78.00
Cassino (one day)	€44.50
Entrance to Museo di Cassino	*€10.00*
Salerno and Paestum	€42.00
Entrance to Templi	*€6.00*
Entrance to Museo	*€4.00*
Pompeii (half day)	€36.00
Entrance to Pompeii Scavi	*€13.00*

Ercolano (Herculaneum) (half day)	€36.00
Entrance to Ercolano Scavi	*€11.00*
Ischia Gardens	€80.00
Entrance to Giardini Mortella	*€12.00*
Vesuvio (half day)	€32.00
Entrance to Vesuvio	*€10.00*
Due Golfi Train Tour	€20.00
Transfer	*€10.00*
Sorrento Musical	€25.00
Sorrento Cooking School	€80.00
Pompeii and Ercolano Select	€110.00
Entrance to Pompeii Scavi	*€13.00*
Entrance to Ercolano Scavi	*€11.00*
Pompeii and wine tasting select	€99.00
Entrance to Pompeii Scavi	*€13.00*
Discover Capri by boat	
Reductions for ages 3 to 9	
Available every day	
01 April 2016 to 31 May 2016	€90.00

| 01 June 2016 to 15 September 2016 | €100 |
| 16 September 2016 to 08 October 2016 | €90.00 |

Discover Positano and Amalfi

Reductions for ages 3 to 9

Available Monday and Wednesday to Saturday

25 April 2016 to 31 May 2016	€100.00
01 June 2016 to 15 September 2016	€110.00
16 September 2016 to 08 October 2016	€100.00

Pompeii and Vesuvius by boat

Available every day

| 15 April 2016 to 31 October 2016 | €69.00 |

Pompeii and Capri by boat

Reductions for ages 3 to 9

| Available Monday to Saturday | €130.00 |

You can find Goldentours at *Via degli Aranci, 25/b*

Phone +39 081 878 10 42.

Their website is: http://www.goldentours.it/en/

An alternative to going on an excursion is to use a

chauffeur service. Goldentours offer this. Other companies are shown on:

http://www.sorrentotourism.com/en/auto-scooter-and-bike-rentals.php

Sorrento Musical

The musical is held at the *Teatro Tasso* in *Piazza San Antonino* (www.teatrotasso.com). You can have dinner and the show or just the show. The show starts after dinner, so that's at 9.30pm. It's a 75 minute show of four scenes, and tells the story of the daily life of the people. It includes folk dancing (the *Tarantella*) and the popular Neapolitan songs.

I haven't seen the show, but reports are good, except for one or two folk who seemed surprised that the show was in Italian. For the benefit of folk who want to know what is going on, you can read all about it at

http://www.teatrotasso.com/tasso_2006/english/show/musical.asp

Or you can just sit back and enjoy the music and the spectacle.

This is an extract from the *Teatro Tasso* website

> "In the first scene featuring the sea. The view is that of the Gulf of Marina Grande to Punta Scutolo: on this stretch of water, fishermen are getting ready to fish daily, making nice with singing and dancing their hard work.

Immediately after the market is shown that the sounds of chatter and gossip, flirtations and quarrels of the intertwined stories of love and jealousy just born with the rhythm and steps of the Tarantella.

Vesuvius silhouetted on the horizon at dusk we entry into the third scene where we can not sing anything but love. The places that have inspired and captivated all cultured travelers of the Grand Tour (from Goethe to Wagner) give off their charm unchanged through songs written in these places.

The last scene of the musical recreates the popular movement of the party. Daylight in the square, while in the sky, you can draw the trails of the fireworks, everyone let grasp the rhythm of dancing and singing their joy of life ready to face the next day, another day of love and work."

A travel company rep assured me that there was no problem taking photos during the show. At the box office they told me that photography was not allowed.

The Sorrento Musical costs €25 if you book directly with the theatre or one of the ticket offices.

Learn To Cook

There is a cookery school at *Viale dei Pini, 52*, in Sant'Agnello. Phone 081.878.32.55 Get there on the *Circumvesuviana*.

In about three hours with lunch you will learn how to prepare a meal for the typical Italian Mediterranean cuisine. Have your photo taken in a chef's hat. See what a mess you can make. You can check the web site at:

http://www.esperidi.com/index.php/en/sorrento-cooking-school-italy

For more sites also see:

http://www.sorrentotourism.com/en/cooking-schools.php

You can also combine your cookery with learning the language.

Learn The Language

Instead of wasting your time on riotous living, you could always learn Italian. OK maybe that's not what you intended to do when you came on holiday, but have you considered going to Sorrento just for that purpose? What better way to learn a language than to immerse yourself in it?

The *Sant'Anna Institute-Sorrento Lingue (SASL)* offers courses throughout the year. It has a campus with dormitories for up to 50 students. It's at *Via Marina Grande, 16*, formerly a convent.

Courses are suitable for students of all ages, nationalities and levels.

Their web site is:

http://www.sorrentolingue.com/index.html

They are represented abroad by Apple Languages.

Their web site is:

http://www.applelanguages.com/en/about/about-apple.php

Get Married

Weddings are regular events in Sorrento. In two weeks of my last visit I chanced across three weddings there. The ceremony is held in the *Chiostro di San Francesco* (the Cloisters of St Francis), and it would be hard to find a more romantic setting. Imagine an oasis of peace, open to the blue skies, walls clad in bougainvillea, with a harp playing gently through the service. It's at once informal, friendly and beautiful. What's not to like about this?

So if you can't think of anything else to do, why not get married, or renew your vows? It's not a spur of the minute thing though - you will need to start planning several months in advance. You will have to ensure that the date you want is available, and so is accommodation for yourself and your guests.

The wedding is a civil ceremony, said to be legal throughout the world, and is available in other resorts in the area as well as Sorrento. You could also choose Positano, Amalfi, Ravello, Praino, and Capri. There are no residency restrictions other than the four and eight days mentioned below.

To help you with your thoughts I've listed some of what is involved. Only take the following as a guide. It's essential to get the legalities right. There will be more requirements, and as these change you really need professional advice. The travel companies can help with this, and so can independent planners. Search on the Internet for "Weddings in Italy."

<u>Things you will need to consider are</u>

- Will you need special wedding insurance in addition to normal travel insurance?
- Will you need a hairdresser and beautician?
- Do you want transport, and if so do you prefer a conventional taxi, a vintage car or a horse-drawn carriage?
- Do you want buttonholes, bouquets or posies for yourselves and guests?
- Do you want a reception, wine and a wedding cake?
- Will photographs taken by guests be sufficient, or will you require the services of a local photographer?
- At the service, do you want music? You could choose a mandolin, guitar or harp. You could probably choose a full size symphony orchestra if you like as the acoustics are excellent, and concerts are regularly held here. But maybe that would be a bit over the top for what is essentially a simple service.
- The ceremony is conducted in Italian. An interpreter is advisable.
- It's an Italian custom to give small gifts to guest. These are known as *favours* or *bombonieres*. Traditionally they are gifts of five almonds symbolising health, happiness, fertility, long life and prosperity.
- There are fees to pay for the service and the venue.

- Will you need extra copies of your wedding certificate? It's bilingual.

Then there are the formalities

- The minimum age is 18.
- You will have to travel under the name on your passport and travel documents. It's essential that your name on all documents is exactly as shown in your passport. If you are changing your name on marriage, you will need to do this on your return.
- You need to stay in the resort for four days before the wedding, excluding your day of arrival, weekends and bank holidays.
- You must also stay in the resort for a minimum of eight days.

Some documents are required

- Full 10 year British passport valid for six months beyond the end of your stay
- Your original Birth Certificate
- If divorced, you need your original Decree Absolute and previous Marriage Certificate. You must wait 300 days (about 10 months) after divorce to remarry.
- If widowed, you will need your late spouse's Death Certificate and previous Marriage Certificate.
- You will require a Certificate of No Impediment from your local Registry Office stating that there is no known impediment to your proposed marriage. This can take up to 23 days to be issued, and must

be issued within six months of the wedding date (3 months in Scotland).

- If you were adopted you will need your original Adoption Certificate.
- If you have changed your name you will need the original Deed Poll notice.

Having read all this, don't despair. Use a holiday company. I've spoken to several people who have been married in Sorrento, and without exception they have said that all the hassle has been removed. Everything has gone smoothly. They have left everything in the hands of the professionals, who have arranged everything. They will tell you what they need, and when they need it. Their wedding coordinator in the resort supervises everything.

It's a common enough site to see the couple walking through the Public Gardens, or posing for photographs in the *Piazza della Vittoria*. They often turn up in the evening at the *Circolo dei Forestieri* to dance the night away. Well some of it.

One final thought. When you receive your wedding certificate, check all the details carefully while you are still in the resort.

REFRESHMENTS

Coffee to the Italians means a strong black espresso. If this is not what you want, then you'll have to be more precise. A small coffee but not quite as strong is a caffe lungo. A large cup of black coffee is a caffe americano, while a large cup of white coffee is a cappuccino.

Sitting at a table costs more than eating and drinking at the bar.

Bars and Restaurants

Bars and restaurants are everywhere, pretty much wherever you go.

Italians tend to eat out on the late side, so expect restaurants to get busy from 9pm onwards.

If you want to dine and watch the *passeggiata*, there's probably no better place than any of those in *Piazza Tasso* itself. There are bars everywhere here. The *Fauno Bar* is one of them. Dine there inside or out. It's a good place for midday snacks. You can't get nearer to the action than this.

Across the road is the Bar Ercolano which is smaller but looks classier. Although open air, it's more enclosed from the Piazza, so people watching is restricted.

Going along the *Corso Italia* there are several places of note. Possibly the most famous of these is 'O Parrucchiano. The surroundings are spectacular and immaculate, both inside and in the gardens. See it at

http://www.parrucchiano.com/en/

Also on the *Corso* (Corso Italia 55/57) there is the English Inn, which also is OK. From its name it inevitably attracts many English folk, but as part of my enjoyment of Italy is to be among Italians, I have only rarely stopped there. Service was good. Italian beer (*birra*) is more akin to lager, but here you can get English beer. They sell John

Smiths, Strongbow, Carlsberg and Peroni.

A few metres further on than the English Inn and on the other side of the road, is Chaplins Bar. They advertise Caffreys and have others. It's small, and tends to be pretty lively. They have satellite TV with Sky Sports.

I've heard good reports of *Panetteria-Pizzeria Franco* at *Corso Italia265* as being highly deserving of its reputation for good food in very informal surroundings.

The *Via San Cesareo* is the narrow street straight ahead of you as you leave *Tasso*. About 100 yards along, where it opens out into a square, you come to the Bar 2000 opposite the *Sedil Dominova*. They often have live music in the evening here. Sometimes it's a piano, sometimes it's one of the groups that wander around Sorrento stopping at various spots during the evening. On one occasion it was a superb tenor - Enzo Bancone. I bought a tape, but it wasn't as good as his live performance. You can sit here and watch the world passing by.

A little further along *Via San Cesareo* you come to La Lanterna. You can dine inside or out. Out is actually on the *via*, so again you can eat and observe the passers-by. It's at:

http://www.lalanternasorrento.it/en/

Heading down to *Piazza San Antonino,* about five minutes from *Piazza Tasso,* you should look in on the *Circolo dei Forestieri*. It's also known as the Foreigners' Club. It's at *Via L. de Maio, 35*, which runs off the *Piazza*. It was founded by the Tourist Boards of Sorrento and Sant'Agnello to encourage meetings between tourists and residents. It serves snacks or meals from a full menu.

There is live music and dancing every evening.

The huge garden area overlooks the Bay of Naples, the harbour of *Marina Piccola*, and the distant view of Vesuvius. Service is pleasant, with no pressure to drink up and move on. Prices are very reasonable for both drinks and for food. It's a pleasant and quiet place for a midday meal.

By day a light breeze often makes it a little less oppressive than the hot streets of the town. By night the live entertainment, usually by keyboard player and vocalist, make it a lively but enchanting spot. It is a popular venue for wedding parties, which can make it a little crowded on those occasions, but I've never failed to find a table. Their website is:

http://www.circolodeiforestieri.com/en/

The *Ristorante Pizzeria L'Abate* is a friendly bar in *Piazza San Antonino 24*. In conversation with the barman one evening, he asked where we were staying. On hearing that it was the Eden, his sympathy was boundless. "*Mamma Mia!*" he said, holding his nose and making a gesture of pulling a toilet chain. He brought us a free drink in sympathy, and when we were leaving he supplied us with a food parcel of pretzels. In fairness this was a few years ago. It's probably a different barman now. I hope it's a different Eden.

There are several places on *Via Padre Reginaldo. L'Antica Trattoria* is a neighbour of Davide's ice cream place. It's a restaurant with a welcoming ambience. Summer 2016 prices include starters and pasta from €18.00 and main courses from €29.00

You can see a preview at
http://www.lanticatrattoria.com/

Also on *Via Padre Reginaldo Giuliani* is *Bar Monnalisa*. It
has a bar and an impressive array of snacks. It's an
Internet cafe. Have a beer while you check your emails.

You can find the Taverna dell'800 at *Via dell'Accademia
29*. It's on the corner of *Via Tasso*, which is the road that
runs down from the cathedral. Walk down from the
cathedral and you will come to it. I've never been in this
one. I always seemed to be on my way to somewhere else,
or I'd already eaten when I've passed by. I think I've
probably missed something. It gives the impression of
being Italian rather than touristy and seems more like a
pub than a restaurant. Maybe I'm wrong. There's usually
music and it radiates a happy atmosphere. I'll see what it
has to offer next time I'm there.

At *Marina Piccola* there is the *Vela Bianca,* nicely
decorated, air conditioned, and just the thing after a
sweltering day in Capri, or when you've just moored your
yacht and the chef has fallen overboard. Do you want
octopus or squid?

http://www.ristorantevelabianca.com/

Down at the far end of *Marina Grande* you come to Tony's
Beach. We usually gravitate to Tony's whenever we are
down there. It's a snack bar with a decent selection of
meals. It's got the usual collection of sun beds, umbrellas
and deck chairs. There's also a stretch of what passes for
sand. It's a picturesque setting, with fishing boats
providing a backdrop for the bathing area. Beach

equipment can be hired, but many people take their own matting and towels to lie on.

We came across it originally on our first visit to *Marina Grande*, when we were ambushed by Tony himself as we walked by. He greeted us as though we were royalty, personally guided us to our seats and served us with *due cappuccini*. He was such a character that I couldn't resist taking his photo. He was happy to oblige. I framed it, and gave it to him on our next visit. He was completely overcome, and this time the *cappuccini* were free. Regrettably Tony is no longer around. We miss him.

To sit there on a scorching day and watch the Italians at play is infinitely better than sitting in a traffic jam on the M6. The beach is very popular with Italian families, the patrons ranging from toddlers to old folk. As with most nationalities, Italians come in all shapes and sizes, ranging from those who are barely visible when standing sideways, to those of vast proportions, solidly filled with pasta. Size doesn't prevent the most massive of the *signori* from donning a costume and blotting out the sun for all those nearby. Tourists who didn't start their diets soon enough before their holiday needn't worry about how they look in swimsuits.

Whilst the sky and the sea are postcard blue, the beach is not in the same league. The sand is shingly, soft, and of volcanic origin. Wet feet emerging from the sea get covered in the dark sand, making bathers look like refugees from a mud bath. Some bathers fill soft drinks bottles with water and wash their feet when they are sitting down again, on the rocks or the edges of their towels. Little children, with less care for their appearances, who have got wet and then played in the sand, look like mid nineteenth century child chimney sweeps. Fortunately there are showers to convert everyone back to the sort of style that is a part of the Italian way of life.

If you are in Sant'Agnello, one couple told me of a wonderful meal they had in *Donna Rosa,* a family run restaurant with great food and very reasonable prices. It's at *Via Marion Crawford 17* but currently closed

Also in Sant'Agnello the Moon Light at *Via Cappuccini, 68/a* is very good and with reasonable prices too

Sandwiches

You can get a sandwich (*panino*) at a shop on the *Corso Italia* a little way past the English Inn. This is the *Bar Veneruso* on *Corso Italia 43-49*, and it's an excellent place for takeaway snacks. You can dine in at the bar, at tables inside or out, or take it with you. It costs less to take it out. Pay first, then hand over your receipt at the bar.

Cut and paste this link for some photos of the bar:

http://www.google.co.uk/search?q=bar+veneruso+sorre nto&hl=en&tbm=isch&tbo=u&source=univ&sa=X&ei=sC WIUaGTE6Hn4QT4r4HQBA&sqi=2&ved=0CFkQsAQ&biw =738&bih=770

For DIY meals, you can get all you need at the supermarkets. You might also find what you want at:

Alimentari - the grocers

Salumeria - the butchers

Ice Cream

If you want an ice cream you have a wide choice. I've tried many places, but my favourite is Davide Il Gelato, which is pretty famous and deserves to be. It's been around since 1957, and they seem to have got the hang of ice cream making now.

It's in the old town, on *Via Padre Reginaldo_Giuliani*, which is one of the roads that run down from *Corso Italia* to the Hotel Tramontano. The last time I counted the ices there were 48 different flavours on display, although they claim to make 60. You can go through agonies choosing. Decisions, decisions! Try a cornet with two different flavours, sit at an outside table in the shade and watch the world go by. They also sell snacks, milk shakes and fruit juices. And if you want something more exotic, there is a mouth-watering menu. Try not to think about the calories. You are there for pleasure, and you can work it off when you get back home. Maybe.

There is a Gelateria: David at *Via Marziale, 19*, but this is not the same company or owner.

Another place that's highly regarded is Raki Gelato at *Via S Cesario,48*. Their website is: https://rakisorrento.com/

Also worth a visit is Bougainvillea. This is on the *Corso Italia* opposite the English Inn. It also has a wide choice, although the one identified as "English Trifle" is not like any trifle I've ever tasted!

Going in the opposite direction, at *Corso Italia, 172* there is *Pollio Pasticceria_*distinguished by an old fashioned ice cream cart outside. It's between *Piazza Tasso* and *Piazza Lauro*. Nothing wrong with the ice cream or cakes, but it's

not as restful during the day with traffic hurtling past.
There's an elegant tea room upstairs.

PART 2 TRAVEL

General

Times, costs, and even names of the various services change from time to time. There are summer and winter services. The information in this guide can be taken as an indication, but you can always find the current situation on the Information Office website. See:

http://www.sorrentotourism.com

Select ENG from the blue bar near the top of the screen

Click HOW TO GET HERE

Click FULL DIRECTIONS TO PUBLIC TRANSPORT, and then "click here to download the text". This gives you access to bus, train and boat services, timetables and costs.

Buses

Bus stops are *fermata*.

There are two different bus services operating in Sorrento:

EAV

These buses are orange or red. They will take you around the Sorrento communities.

There are five services:

<u>LINE A</u>	Massa Lubrense, Capo di Sorrento, Sorrento town centre, Sant'Agnello, Piano di Sorrento and Meta
<u>LINES B OR C</u>	Piano di Sorrento, Sant'Agnello, Sorrento town centre, and Marina Piccola
<u>LINE E</u>	Marina Grande and Sorrento train station. Along Via degli Aranci and Via Parsano to Hilton Sorrento Palace Hotel

SITA

Buses are red and take you outside the Sorrento communities to Positano and Amalfi. From Amalfi there are other bus services to Agerola or Ravello, or to Atrani, Minori, Maiori, Vietri sul Mare and Salerno.

Another service takes you to Massa Lubrense, Priora, Sant'Agata, Marina Lobra, Nerano, Marina del Cantone and back

Tickets

Tickets for buses are *Unico Campania*. You can get them from *tabacchi* and newsagents.

EAV local buses travel to and within the communities of Sorrento. Tickets are TIC AC and cost € 1.60 valid for 60 minutes. There are five lines:

LINE A   Massa Lubrense, Capo di Sorrento,Sorrento town centre, Sant'Agnello, Piano di Sorrento and Meta

LINES B OR C Piano di Sorrento, Sant'Agnello, Sorrento town centre to

          Marina Piccola

LINE D   Marina Grande to Sorrento town centre

LINE E   Sorrento train station to the Hilton Sorrento Palace Hotel (Via degli

          Aranci and Via Parsano)

For SITA buses

AC 1   € 1.20 Sorrento to Massa Lubrense, Sant'Agata, and Nerano Cantone

AC 2   € 1.80 from Sorrento to Positano

AC 4   € 2.70 from Sorrento to Amalfi or Ravello

AC 5   € 3.10 from Sorrento to Salerno

Costiera Sita Sud daily € 8,00 valid for 24 hours

You must have a ticket before you get on a bus. There are

validating machines on the buses. There are two entrances (*Entrata*) - one at the front near the driver and one at the rear. There is always a machine near the driver, and usually, but not always, one near the rear entrance. Inserting the ticket enters the date and time on the reverse of the ticket. It's essential to have your ticket validated in this way or it will cost you if it's checked.

Once your ticket has been endorsed by the machine, you can use it on any other of the buses so long as your final journey ends before the expiry of the time for which you have bought the ticket. There's no need to put it in a machine again. The ticket can be used only within the Sorrento Peninsula and the Amalfi coast, but this includes all the destinations listed above.

If you get on at the rear and there is no machine, you must endorse the ticket yourself by entering the date and time. So carry a pen.

Trains

The *Circumvesuviana* train runs between Sorrento and Naples, with stops at:

Sant'Agnello

Piano di Sorrento

Vico Equense

Castellammare

Pompeii Scavi

Ercolano Scavi

All trains don't stop at all of the stations.

It's a regular service, starting at 06.09 and running at two or three trains an hour until 21.39. (There are some night time bus services between Sorrento and Naples outside these times.)

You can check the timetable at:

http://www.eavsrl.it/web/sites/default/files/eavferro/ Napoli%20-%20Sorrento_0.pdf

It's also just as well to check your change when you pay for your ticket. I've seen several reports of errors in change. You may be in a hurry to catch a train, and have a queue of people behind you, but still check. It's a good idea to either give the right change, or to use the smallest possible denomination above the expected cost and to be aware of how much change you should receive. Incidentally I have heard similar warnings about Vesuvius, a water seller at Marina Piccola, and in my own experience in Capri. Maybe it's endemic, with tourists seen as an easy option.

The tickets are *Unico Campania* and are available at *tabacchi* and newsagents as well as at the station. You may feel under less pressure if buying from a shop rather than at the station.

When travelling back to Sorrento in the afternoon, take a seat on the left- hand side (facing the direction of travel) to avoid the glare of the sun.

Pity about the graffiti on the trains. You may also be accosted by beggars, usually gypsies. Either ignore them or say *non* (no) as emphatically as you can manage. Don't let them see any signs of a wallet.

Pickpockets sometimes operate on the trains, so ensure that all your belongings and money are secure. If you've got a backpack, hold it in your hand rather than wearing it on your back.

If you find all this a bit off-putting, don't expect any trouble. You are unlikely to have any problems at all. I've got one personal experience that shows that folk on this train are not as bad as they are sometimes made out. When I travelled to Ercolano en route to Vesuvius, my young son left his camera on the train. I reported this at the ticket office immediately. They phoned ahead to Naples. We waited about a half hour, and then to my great surprise the camera came back on another train and was duly presented to my son. Congratulations all round! It was a fairly cheap camera, but even so...

Boats

There are two boat services:

Caremar

They run ferries to Capri. The journey takes 30 minutes by fast ferry and costs €14.80 one way. Their schedule is at: http://www.caremar.it/index.php/en/Timetables/

Gescab

Their boats are Jetfoils and go to Capri in 25 minutes. The fare is €18.30 one way. Napoli in 35 minutes costs €12.30 one way. Ischia in 60 minutes for €40.40 return.

Ferry times to Capri are subject to regular change. Check the times a couple of days before you travel at http://www.capri.com/en/ferry-schedule?path_id=14.

Horse and Carriage

Take a trip round town on a horse and carriage. They start off from Piazza

Tasso. Be sure to check with the driver just where he will take you and at what cost. Do this before climbing aboard.

Taxis

The main taxi rank is at the *Piazza Tasso*. Again, establish costs before you commit. One couple returning to the UK in October 2013 reported being charged €15 for a one mile journey.

As a tourist, the price may be a little inflated. Ask for their best price (*che prezzo puoi farmi?*), and ask them to write it down (*si prega di scrivere*). Produce your own paper and a pen, so they can't avoid knowing what you want.

PART 3 PLACES TO VISIT

The Amalfi Drive

OK, it's not a place, it's a way to get to many places. It's an experience in itself, and one not to be missed.

The Amalfi Drive is world famous. The scenery is breathtaking. The coast road is an engineer's dream and a motorist's nightmare for anyone other than an Italian. If you hire a car, give serious thought to leaving it behind for this trip. If you are driving you won't be able to appreciate the views. You will spend time going backwards in the face of oncoming traffic. As waiting for anything is anathema to an Italian driver, he will seek to pass you as soon as there is a gap equal to two millimetres plus the width of his car. This finely judged driving can knock years off your life and may cost you your wing mirrors. It's a long drop into the sea if it all goes wrong, but the walls are pretty sturdy.

On an organised excursion, for the best views, sit on the right hand side of the coach (i.e. this will be the right hand side as you sit down facing the driver). The excursion usually features a stop on the way, lunch in Amalfi and an afternoon in Ravello.

The road goes from *S Agata sui due Golfi* to *Vietri sul Mare*. This is a 45 mile stretch past some of the most spectacular and dramatic scenery you are likely to come across anywhere. Along the way you will see, look down on, pass by, or stop at some or all of:

Positano

Praiano

Grotta Smeraldo

Conca dei Marini

Amalfi

Atrani

Ravello

Minori

Maiori

Vietri sul Mare

Salerno

Of these, an excursion is likely to make just one stop for a short break at Grotta Smeraldo. Here there is a restaurant, shop, toilets and spectacular views. Then it will continue before reaching the furthest extent of its journey at Amalfi, where you will have time to stop for lunch and to explore its delights before going on to an afternoon in Ravello for even more delights. This is usually the end of organized excursions, although the road continues on to Salerno.

If you would like a preview there is a video of Julia Bradbury on the Amalfi Drive at:

http://www.youtube.com/watch?v=8CCVXMLzGeE

Amalfi

Way back in time (ninth to twelfth centuries.), Amalfi was one of the great Italian Maritime Republics (others were Venice, Genova and Pisa)

You can get to Amalfi by boat (Jetfoil with the Gescab/Alilauro company for €34.00 return) or by SITA bus, but it's one of the times when an excursion, even though it costs more, is worth considering. Then you can enjoy the scenery in comfort and with a commentary from a guide.

If the beaches (or lack of them) in Sorrento were a source of annoyance, you'll be happier here.

Amalfi has a magnificent cathedral (the *Duomo di Sant'Andrea*) dominating the *Piazza Duomo*. Not least impressive are the 62 steps leading up to it, so take a deep breath. It dates back to the ninth century. The bronze doors are a notable feature. They were made in 1066, which is the time when William the Conqueror was making a nuisance of himself at the Battle of Hastings.

The Duomo houses the remains of Sant'Andrew in the crypt. (Don't forget to look up at the ceiling.) In addition to being the patron saint of Amalfi, Saint Andrew also doubles up as the patron saint of Scotland. There is no rest for some folk.

The *Chiostro del Paradiso* (Cloister of Paradise) is well worth a visit. You can take a tour starting here and including the Duomo.

Remember to wear acceptable clothing.

The little Church of St. Mary's Square (*Chiesa di S. Maria a Piazza*) in the underpass between *Piazza Flavio Gioia* and *Piazza Duomo* bears a plaque that says: *"Il giorno dell giudizio, per gli Amalfitani che andranno in paradiso, sara un giorno come tutti gli altri"* This translates as "The Day of Judgement, for the people of Amalfi, which will go to Heaven will be a day like any other". That probably says it all.

Capri

This is one of three islands in the Bay of Naples, the other two being Ischia and Procida. It isn't visible from Sorrento, not because of distance but because the headland gets in the way. (You can see the other two islands.)

Booking a return doesn't save money, but it does save you having to queue again in Capri to book your journey back to Sorrento. On the other hand it's quite possible that when you are ready to return, the next boat may belong to another company. My preference would always be to book single and return at the time that's most suitable for me.

The fare for the boat is €14.80 single. If you are carrying luggage, there is an additional charge of €2 for each suitcase. If you book return, a return time will be shown on the ticket. Check that you will be able to return at other times if you wish, although still with the same company.

The approach to Capri is pretty spectacular and worth a photo or two if you can get to the open air. It wouldn't be so good through the windows of the faster boats.

Marina Grande is the main port and is where the boats come in. It differs from Sorrento in that *Marina Grande* really is the big one. There's also a *Marina Piccola* on the other side of the island.

The harbour area is thronged with taxi drivers hawking for custom. The taxis are open top and with a canopy over to provide shade. Before succumbing to these offers you should know what you want to see, and agree the fare beforehand. Have some paper handy - pretend you don't understand what he is saying and ask him to write the cost down (*quanto costa?*). Make sure that the return journey (*ritorno*) is included, and that he will wait while you look at the things of interest to you. Haggling is not only permissible, but expected.

The harbour area itself is of limited interest and you will want to make your way to some of the attractions of the island.

You can go up to Capri Town on foot if you wish, but it can be a bit wearing. Most people choose to go up on the funicular. There will probably be a queue. The funicular railway (*funicolare*) takes you up the steep incline between the port and Capri Town. It consists of two cars which counterbalance each other, one going up as the other comes down. They run on a single track with a passing place in the middle. You emerge at the top into the *Piazzetta (Piazza Umberto I)*.

Tickets for both the funicular and for the bus to Anacapri are available from the ticket office to your right as you emerge from the Marina. Tickets for the funicular cost €1.80 single. The bus to Anacapri costs the same. Return costs are double. Beware. I didn't check my change until I was in the queue for the funicular and found that I had

been short changed by €5.00. Maybe it was a genuine
mistake. The prices are displayed. Just check the price
and make sure that another mistake doesn't happen to
you. Return to Anacapri is a good idea, but consider single
only for the funicular. Going down on foot is both
reasonably easy and interesting. The path is pedestrian
only, and passes some lovely villas on the way. In peak
holiday times it can be quicker coming down on foot than
waiting for a place on the funicular.

An alternative to the funicular is to go by bus. From just a
few steps past the ticket office, you can take a bus to Capri
Town or Anacapri. You can pay the driver.

Capri Town

The Town can be uncomfortably busy, particularly in the
Piazzetta.

The Town itself is full of classy but expensive shops. You
can find all the designer labels here, with matching prices.
Just about everything costs more than in Sorrento.

Anacapri

Buses to Anacapri are only two or three minutes' walk to
the right from the top of the funicular. If you didn't book
your bus ticket at the same time as the funicular, be sure
to get it at the nearby office before boarding the bus.

A slight surprise here is that Capri has discovered queues,
and you will need to follow the barriers round to the
Anacapri bus. Timetables are not evident, the bus going
when full. Full has a different meaning on Capri than
elsewhere in the civilised world. If it is humanly possible
to shoehorn another person aboard, then this will be

done. Journey time is about 10 minutes, but it will feel longer!

Although apparently full to capacity at the start of the journey, this won't prevent the bus from stopping further along to pick up yet more passengers. The congestion is mind boggling. Togetherness takes on a whole new meaning. This jamming of bodies together has the advantage of making it totally impossible for anyone to fall down as the driver makes the spectacular ascent along the narrow, twisting road with multiple hairpins that leads to Anacapri. Whilst thus compressed, you can look out of the window and see just how far down it will be if the driver makes a mistake. More positively, you can admire either the view or your neighbour's armpit as he clings on. If you happen to have your nose flattened against the driver's compartment you can watch as he drives with one hand around the hairpins, the other being used for the incessant gear changes.

Anacapri, when you get there, is worth the journey. It is a town of sparkling cleanliness. All the buildings seem to have been newly painted white that very morning, and dazzle in the sun. The white is contrasted by the blue of the sky and the purple of the bougainvillea.

The main stop for the bus is at the *Piazza Vittoria*. At the top of the steps is the *Mariorita* store. It's worth going in as it's air conditioned. It stocks clothing from many of the top fashion names - Versace, Hugo Boss, Moschino and Armani, to name but a few. It also stocks many luxury items - glassware, leather, shoes and more. It can seriously damage your holiday budget.

A visit to the top of *Monte Solaro* may be worth the effort taking the path, but most people settle for less effort and choose the chairlift (*la seggiovia*). It leaves from the piazza. They are single seats. The fare is €10.00 (return!). The place to stand is clearly marked on the ground, and an attendant helps passengers on and flicks the safety bar over. The safety bar is hinged on the left and comes down with a satisfying thud, so keep any cameras well out of the way, on your left hand side.

It takes just 12 minutes of total peace, broken only by the periodic clatter when going past the supporting pylons. In places your feet are almost touching the vegetation.

At the top you may find many butterflies, and the views down to the *Faraglioni Rocks* are stunning. There are three rocks, the highest being a spectacular 111m high.

You can get refreshments at the top, or have a picnic if you have brought your own stuff.

If you have the time you might like to walk back down to Anacapri. Follow the signs for the **Cetrella Hermitage**, but if it's hot, the chairlift will probably beckon again. To be honest I wouldn't consider anything else.

If you are in need of refreshment you could call in at the Capri Palace. They have a lovely terrace where you can sit and enjoy coffee, served with a small fruit tart.

The only disadvantage of going up to Anacapri is that you have to go back down again, repeating the pleasures of the upward journey, but this time gravity assisted for even more speed. Return buses from the piazza can be fairly full on arrival. The obvious thing to do is to walk back to the previous stop and board the bus there. The road is the *Viale De Tommaso*. It's not far and will only take a couple of minutes. You may even get a seat!

Villa San Michele

The villa is in Anacapri, just a short walk from the bus stop. It goes past a line of shops, mostly expensive. It's worth the walk, even if you don't go into the villa. Entrance to the Villa is €7.00.

The villa was built by Dr. Axel Martin Fredrik Munthe (1857-1949). He was Swedish court physician. He practiced as a physician and psychiatrist in Paris and Rome. He retired to Capri where he built the villa. He wrote "The Story of San Michelle" (1929), about his life and the building of his villa on the island. It was a best-seller. It's a good read.

The views down from just past the villa are of the island and across the bay to the Sorrentine peninsula beyond.

Blue Grotto (Grotta Azzurra)

The Blue Grotto is the one you hear about, but there are two other grottos on the island - the *Grotta Verde* (green) and the *Grotta Bianca* (white).

You can get to it from *Marina Grande* by a cruise round the island, stopping at the Grotto, or by boat just to the Grotto. You can also go by bus from Anacapri. The stop is 50m from *Piazza Vittoria*. You can also walk there. It's 3.5km from the centre of Anacapri.

Entrance to the Grotto is by rowing boat. If arriving by sea, you are transferred to a rowing boat. If by road you can join the queue and a boat will pick you up from there.

The rowing boat will take you to another boat with a cash register for you to pay the €13 entrance fee. The entrance to the Grotto is only about a metre high, sometimes less depending on sea conditions. You will have to lie down as you pass through.

The blue effect is most spectacular between 12.00 and 14.00. It may disappoint you on a cloudy day. Before boarding your ship again, the oarsman expects a tip.

Villa Jovis

The Villa Jovis was a residence of the Emperor Tiberius. It's about a 45 minute walk from *Piazza Umberto* in Capri Town to the ruins of the villa, which was reputedly the scene of grand scale Roman orgies, with those out of favour taking the direct route to the base of the cliff, but these stories have since been discounted.

Gracie Fields Villa

Gracie Fields was a Lancashire lass from Rochdale with a lovely voice. She made many films. She was a big name in the 1930s and was one of the highest paid stars of her day, but tarnished her image when she married an Italian citizen (film director Monty Banks) during the war. She eventually settled in Capri. Not a bad swap, some might think. Among her famous songs were "Sally" and "The Biggest Aspidistra in the World." They don't write them like that any more. She died in 1979. She is buried in the non-Catholic cemetery near her home.

Her home in Capri (*La Canzone Del Mare*) has views of *Marina Piccola* and the *Faraglioni* rocks.

Caserta

If you are taking an excursion you will probably find that Caserta and Cassino are part of the same outing. Caserta is about 60km from Sorrento.

If you are feeling independent you can get the Circumvesuviana to Naples and then a train from *Napoli Centrale* station to Caserta. The station in Caserta is only a few minutes' walk from the Royal Palace.

This Palace is the main attraction in Caserta. It's a magnificent building that was built in the 18th century by Charles III (King Carlo III), a Bourbon king. It has more than 1200 rooms, and is lavishly decorated. The gardens extend to 3km and are stunningly beautiful. They feature pools and fountains, and a 75m waterfall that is visible from the palace.

Building the palace was an attempt to rival or better Versailles. Shows what you can do if you are jealous and have money.

The size of this place is mind boggling. The 1200 rooms feature1790 windows and 34 staircases. During the war, from 1943, it was the headquarters of the Allied Forces. There are stories of them driving along the corridors in a Jeep.

On 29 April 1945 the surrender of the German army in Italy was accepted here.

Cassino

Cassino is quite a bit further on from Caserta, being about 150km from Sorrento. It is the site of a famous abbey, founded in 529 by St. Benedict. It was destroyed in the Second World War during the battle of *Monte Cassino*. It has since been faithfully restored.

On a personal note, my uncle was in the army and was very seriously wounded during the battle. As he lay in a shell hole he saw two German soldiers appear. He waited for them to lob a hand grenade in. Instead they picked him up and carried him between them for a considerable distance over rocky terrain to their base hospital, from where he was sent on to Germany where skilled surgeons rebuilt his face.

After recovering he spent the rest of the war in a prisoner of war camp with guards who were friendly and compassionate. He had nothing but good to say of the Germans who came his way and saved his life, and of his subsequent treatment.

A British and Commonwealth war cemetery is there as the final resting place for those who fought in the battle

Herculaneum

Herculaneum is only about a third of the size of Pompeii, so it's easier to get round it all. It also attracts fewer visitors, so it's much less crowded. Much of what was Herculaneum is now covered by the town of Ercolano. It was rediscovered in 1709.

Like Pompeii, it was a victim of the eruption of Vesuvius.

This was on August 25 AD79, the day after Pompeii was engulfed. On the first day of the eruption Herculaneum only suffered a few centimetres of ash, but on the second day it was hit by a deadly pyroclastic flow of toxic gas, ash and stone. The temperature of 500C killed instantly, and not very pleasantly. It vaporised the flesh and caused the brain to swell, thus cracking the skulls. Only skeletons remained, so in this respect it differed from Pompeii. Wood was carbonised. You can see this in the exhibits that are on view. Herculaneum was covered to a depth of 25 metres.

The last figures I heard were that 340 skeletons had been recovered from the boat sheds, where most of the people remaining in Herculaneum had taken shelter and died.

An organised half day excursion to Herculaneum costs €36.00. Alternatively you can get a *Circumvesuviana* train to *Ercolano Scavi* for €2.70 (*Scavi* means excavation). Journey time is about 40 minutes from Sorrento.

Entry to the site is €11 but is free for EU citizens under 18. Take your passports as proof of age.

You can take a bus from the station to the site.

Ischia

Ischia (pronounced *Isskeea*) is the largest island in the Gulf of Naples. It has a mountainous interior. The highest point is *Monte Epomeo* at 788m (2580ft). It is an extinct volcano.

Arriving on an excursion you will have a choice of landing and going for a coach trip around the island, or staying on board for a cruise along the coast and then mooring at sea for swimming and to await the return of the coach travellers.

Ischia is renowned for its thermal springs. There are said to be over a hundred of them, varying in temperature from 15 to 86 Centigrade. So you can emerge lightly poached. You can also have a mud bath. This could be quite nostalgic for people used to going to music festivals in the UK. If you really want to be pampered, the highest rated establishment is *Spa Manzi* in *Casamicciola*

http://www.termemanzihotel.com/

Giardini La Mortella is a spectacular botanical garden at *Forio*. It was created by Lady Susana Walton, wife of Sir William Walton, the British composer. There are many hundreds of different plants. A TV documentary suggested 1000. A bus runs to the garden from the port. Entrance is €12.00 or €10.00 for those under 18 or over 70. The walk up to the gardens is steep.

The Garden is open to the public from March 26 to November 1 on Tuesday, Thursday, Saturday and Sunday from 9 am to 7 pm (ticket offices close at 6 pm)

Additional opening days in 2016are:

- Monday March 28 - Easter Monday (from 9 am to 5 pm)

- Monday October 31 (from 9 am to 5 pm)

Naples

Naples is the capital city of Campania. There are many books extolling the virtues of Naples. Some of its attractions are world famous. To name but a few, you can see the *San Carlo* opera house, the cathedral (on *Via del Duomo*), and the National Archaeological Museum in *Piazza Museo Nazionale*.

Get there by boat (Gescab) for €12.30, by *Circumvesuviana* train for €3.60 or on an organised excursion.

The Secret Room

The museum houses treasures from the excavations of Pompeii and Herculaneum. Most are on public view, but if you want to see the lack of inhibitions of the locals you can ask to see the secret room (*Gabinetto Segreto*). You will have to go to the Information Desk where you will be given an admission voucher and a time for your visit. It's free. You are allowed 45 minutes, and you can take photographs but you must not use flash. Be aware of this if you have a compact camera that automatically uses flash, and do whatever you need to do to suppress it.

If you want a preview, there is a short video at

http://www.youtube.com/watch?v=X4LKIOgqLSo

Ceremony of San Gennaro

San Gennaro (St Januarius) is the patron saint of Naples. He was the Bishop of Benevento. The Romans were giving Christians a hard time in AD305. St Januarius was first consigned to a furnace, from which he emerged unscathed. Next it was into the arena with wild animals, who knelt at his feet. Running out of options, Timothy, governor of Campania, settled for beheading, and this time it worked.

A flask of his blood was saved, and this is held in two phials which are paraded and brought to the altar of the cathedral. These ceremonies are held three times a year, on the Saturday before the first Sunday in May, on the anniversary of his martyrdom on19 September, and on 16 December in commemoration of an eruption of Mt Vesuvius in 1631 in which the saint was believed to have intervened.

If the blood liquefies, it's a good omen that all will be well for Naples in the coming months. This usually happens quite quickly, but can sometimes take hours, or even days. Success is signalled by the waving of a white handkerchief. If it fails to liquefy, then bad times are believed to be in store, and all is doom and gloom. Napoli may lose a few matches. Usually all is well, but disasters have reportedly occurred on at least five occasions when the blood has failed to liquefy.

The phials have been examined by Italian scientists who confirm that they do contain blood. There are many theories about the liquefaction, but it still remains unexplained by science and as a miracle for the faithful.

There is a story that during the war a German officer said that someone would be shot if the miracle didn't happen. It did.

You can watch a video of the ceremony that was held on 19 September 2011. It's on YouTube at

http://www.youtube.com/watch?v=0MTrKHXvfCs
&feature=youtu.be&t=2m55s

But...

I must tell you why you might consider giving Naples a
miss. In spite of all that this once beautiful city has to
offer, it wouldn't take you long to discover that traffic in
Naples has its own rules. Traffic lights are irrelevant.
Drivers are competitive. Pedestrians are expendable. But
more importantly, Naples is a city in the grip of the
Camorra. The Camorra is seriously bad news. They are
into protection, extortion, drugs, racketeering and waste
disposal. There is more about the Camorra later.

Tour guides will warn you not to take anything of value,
women to remove jewellery, expensive cameras not to be
on view, leave expensive watches behind.

On an early visit to Sorrento I was told of a large
American who was warned not to wear his Rolex watch
on his visit. "I've travelled the world wearing this watch,
and I'm not taking it off to go to Naples," he said. In due
course he and his wife were enjoying a cup of coffee at an
outside table when they were approached by two
Neapolitans. One thumped him on the arm, presumably to
deaden it, and the other went for his watch. His arm
wasn't deadened. He got hold of one of them and
proceeded to beat his head on the table. The other fled.
But the most revealing thing about this episode was that
no one sitting at adjoining tables paid any attention to it.
It was just a part of everyday life to them.

On my last visit to Sorrento a woman guest at my hotel
was walking on the pavement in Naples. Two guys on a
scooter mounted the pavement, hooking the handlebar of

their scooter into the strap of her shoulder bag and driving off, taking the bag with them and leaving her face down on the pavement. She wasn't seriously hurt, but could have been. But she was shocked, and her holiday spoiled.

Camorra

No information about Naples would be complete without a mention of the Camorra.

There is a saying: "See Naples and die". Regrettably this is a saying that can be all too true. The murder rate is high. It's the home of the Camorra, the local branch of the Mafia, now regarded as being much bigger than the Sicilian Mafia.

The Camorra is a lethal bunch. There are several different clans, with a propensity for shooting each other. They have killed more than the Sicilian Mafia, more than the IRA in Ireland, and more than ETA in Spain.

Camorra influence in and around Naples has led to problems with refuse collection, which seems to be under their control. Landfill sites are full, so plastic bags of rubbish abound at the roadside, many split and their contents spread around.

Possibly even worse than the piles of rubbish is the serious problem of what the Camorra is doing to the countryside. Toxic waste is being buried and the toxins are leaking into the environment, affecting both dairy farming, agriculture, and the health of the people.

There can be few businesses that don't make regular contributions to the various clans. Buy a cappuccino and the chances are that you are making a small contribution to their immense wealth. Little stops them, and nothing is sacred. Father Peppino Diana was a parish priest who campaigned against the Mafia. He was murdered in his own church in 1994. They have total control of some areas of Naples. You won't see anything of them if you stick to the tourist areas, but that doesn't mean that local riff-raff won't be around and capable of intruding on your life. Not least of them are the teams of pickpockets. They run a slick operation, so beware of crowded places.

When driving through the fringes of Naples once, the coach I was on paused briefly and I could see, in an upstairs room, a very large guy beating up a much smaller one. It spoiled a sunny day for me. I don't suppose it did much for him either.

On another occasion during my research in Sorrento I was recording a fact-finding chat in a shop. It was very informative until I asked about the Camorra. My interviewee and her companion exchanged glances. The conversation stopped. Maybe the walls have ears.

I had never heard any suggestion of Camorra activity in Sorrento so I was a little surprised. But one experience maybe showed an unhealthy intrusion into Sorrento. When my wife goes to the market, I normally take refuge in the cemetery. It's such a tranquil spot in complete contrast to the market.

Periodically, remains are taken from their burial in the ground and the casks transferred to positions in the walls fronted by memorial stones bearing their names. On one occasion I was walking along an aisle between rows of these memorials when I came across one that had been smashed and the cask revealed inside.

I went to the office at the entrance of the cemetery and tried to explain what I had seen, but this isn't the sort of event that's covered in the phrase books. My Italian wasn't up to it, and they had no idea what I was talking about. I went back, took a video and replayed it to them. I've never seen such a change in people. I led one of them back to show the place and left him to it, but I couldn't escape the feeling that this area of peacefulness had been touched by something evil.

It seems that there's no rest even when you are dead for some people.

If you want to learn more about the Camorra, there is an excellent but disturbing book about them. It's *Gomorrah - Italy's Other Mafia* by Roberto Saviano.

Take precautions

You have to ask yourself if this is the place for you. If you do decide to go, try not to identify yourself as a target. Easier said than done if you have white legs ending in black socks in sandals. You'll never look like a Neapolitan, but at least try to look like a world savvy traveller. And standing there with a map in your hand won't give that image. Try to decide where you want to go before getting to Naples, so you've at least got some idea of the route you will be following.

Heed the warnings, only take the money you need, don't have it all in one pocket, keep any high denomination notes in the most secure spot you've got, don't carry a shoulder bag or handbag on the road side of the pavement, have a bag strap over your head rather than just on the shoulder, don't put bags, cameras or smartphones on tables or chairs - rather keep them on your lap, preferably with your hand on them.

Backpacks - the name tells it all. If it's on your back, you can't see what is happening behind you, and don't think you would feel it if someone decided to help themselves to the contents. There's a particular risk of your load being lightened on buses, trains, or anywhere where there is a bit of a crush.

Another trick is to slit open your handbag. Keep your hand on your bag as you walk around. Granted you could lose your fingers that way, but surgeons can do wonders nowadays.

Children are not all innocent and harmless, often operating in pairs or groups, and if one of them manages to make off with your wallet, you probably wouldn't get it back by chasing after him - he'll have passed it on to someone else almost immediately, although you may get some satisfaction from bouncing him up and down.

Be aware of all that is going on around you, realise that any nearby distractions may be being put on for your benefit, accept that the pickpockets are very accomplished, above all, be vigilant, and good luck!

Chances are that you will find it a rewarding experience. Most people do. But if you are robbed, report it to the police in Naples. Police back in Sorrento can only deal with crime in Sorrento itself.

Paestum

In excursions, Paestum is part of an outing that also includes Salerno. It's

98km from Sorrento.

Paestum was founded by the Greeks in 650BC. It later became a Roman colony, but was eventually abandoned.

The Greek legacy is three temples:

- The oldest is the Temple of Hera, built around 530BC.
- The Temple of Ceres dates back to about 500BC.
- Most impressive is the Temple of Neptune. It was built about 450BC. It is one of the best preserved in Europe.

There is a fine museum within the grounds.

Pompeii

A trip to Pompeii is often combined with a visit to Vesuvius. This makes for a pretty hectic day, especially if it's hot. Pompeii is big, and Vesuvius is high.

If you want to go by *Circumvesuviana* train, the station you want is *Pompei Scavi*. The site entrance is only a short walk from the station. The fare is €2.20

Entry to Pompeii is €11.00. Free for EU citizens under 18. Take your passports as proof of age.

There is little shade as you walk round here, so a hat is a good idea. So is a bottle of water. Good shoes, too. Forget the high heels.

If you are interested in cameos, there is a cameo factory at Pompeii where they give instructive talks. The first cameos were made in the area around Pompeii.

Remember that their value is not based on size or colour - only on the workmanship. There are toilets in the building - no charge.

Pompeii was a commercial centre, unlike Herculaneum, which was residential. During the eruption of AD79 it was covered in stones and ash, but it was the pyroclastic flow that killed the people. Pompeii is 5km further from Vesuvius than Herculaneum, so the temperature is estimated to have fallen from 500C to 300C. This temperature was enough to kill instantly, but not to incinerate the skin or clothes. This seems hard to credit, but has since been proved experimentally

The eruption was preceded by earth tremors, but these were not taken as a warning of the impending disaster. The residents didn't know that it was a volcano - it had been quiet for seven centuries.

The remains were discovered around 1750. The most important finds were taken to the museum in Naples.

The figures you can see are neither statues nor the remains of people. The people died in the pyroclastic flow. The shower of ash that enveloped their bodies was so fine that it clung to every crease and fold and expression, so it showed details of their features and the clothes they wore. Eventually it set like cement. Over time the flesh decayed, leaving only an imprint of the body in the cavity. When the cavities were discovered, they were filled with plaster. So what you see are casts that capture the moment of death.

During your tour you are likely to come across evidence that many of the residents led uninhibited lives. The tour guides tend to explain what you can see with great relish, so parents may get some searching questions afterwards from their children. Get ready to distract them before the detail gets too graphic.

If you are really into this, there are books on erotic Pompeii. And if you go to the National Archaeological Museum in spite of the warning about visits to Naples, once inside you can ask to see the secret room (*Gabinetto Segreto*). There is more about this in the section on Naples.

If you want to take a memorable photo, try the view from the Temple of Jupiter with Vesuvius providing the backdrop.

Positano

If you arrived in Positano by sea you will have passed the little islands just off the coast. They are the *Le Galli*. They are privately owned. The largest of these was once owned by Rudolf Nureyev, the Russian ballet dancer.

You can stay on *Li Galli*, but it won't come cheap. Contact Bellini Travel at

www.bellinitravel.com

According to legend, the islands were once mermaids. They were turned into the islands by Ulysses. This was a pretty high price to pay for singing to him. Lucky that Ulysses is not a judge on the X Factor show on television.

You have to wonder why anyone in their right mind would have built a town here.

Insanity seems to be the likeliest reason. Any sane person

would have looked at the cliff face and gone somewhere else. But mad or not, the result is an impossibly spectacular vertical town. The colourful houses cling to the cliff face and hotel porters face imminent heart attacks transporting luggage up endless steps.

According to Vanessa (see Acknowledgements) there are 777 steps up to the cemetery in Positano. It's a wonder that anyone ever gets to graveside. If you really want to upset your relatives, you could ask to be buried there.

Positano is not offered as a guided tour, but is easy to reach independently, and is well worth a visit, especially for the ladies as it's full of boutiques selling a huge choice of clothes, but not cheaply. Indeed, I was barely off the boat before a girl went past wearing a T-shirt "Official Shopping T-Shirt. Born to Spend." She had come to the right place.

You can go by road, taking the SITA bus, or by Jetfoil with the Gescab/Alilauro company . Bus is cheaper, and you can see something of the wonders of the Amalfi Drive. Positano is on the way to Amalfi. But you are enclosed in the bus, you may have to stand, and the bus won't stop and wait to allow you to enjoy the views. There are two bus stops. The first is quite a way from the centre. The second one, on the way to Praiano is walking distance from the centre.

Going by boat from Sorrento costs €32 return but the journey is enjoyable, you get the sea air and the sunshine, and the scene as you approach Positano is absolutely spectacular. Also you are in the midst of it all as soon as you land, and there's nothing like the chaos that you will meet in Capri, so it's simple to locate your boat on the return journey.

As you approach from the sea, one of the most striking views is the majolica dome of the *Chiesa Santa Maria dell'Assunta*. On a hot day it's lovely and cool inside the church.

Procida

Procida (pronounced *Procheeda*) is the smallest of the Neapolitan islands and is about 3 miles from Ischia. It's about 4 square kilometres in size.

There is no direct sailing there from Sorrento. You have to go via Naples, Pozzuoli or Ischia. Ischia is the best bet as you can then see both islands. It's also visited by some cruises.

Procida has a sea front like a film set. From the sea it gives the appearance of there being nothing behind it. When I visited it some years ago there was a sunken ship in the harbour that looked as though it had been there for many years. With the Italian motto seemingly being *domani* (tomorrow), no doubt it will be there for many years to come.

The impressive castle (Terra Murata) was built in 1563 by Innico D'Avalos, of a very noble Neapolitan family with Spanish origins. It was a prison for 150 years but has been closed for some time now. Its destiny is yet to be decided but there is talk of it becoming a conference centre or a hotel. This upsets the islanders, who might prefer a prison to what may replace it and bring more visitors.

Ravello

This place is beautiful. You really shouldn't miss it. It's 367m above sea level and commands outstanding views both down to the sea, and to the countryside.

Entry to the grounds of the Villa Rufolo costs €5.00. The gardens here were the inspiration for the Garden of Klingsor in the second act of Richard Wagner's opera Parsifal. On 26th May 1880, Wagner signed the Villa's Visitors' Book, writing "The enchanted garden of Klingsor has been found." In German legend Parsifal was a knight who went in search of the Holy Grail. He was the father of Lohengrin.

Concerts are given here on a platform built out precariously on the cliff, and bad news for any musicians who suffer from vertigo. Not a recommended venue for the 1812 Overture - the final salvos might be too much. A Wagner festival is held every year.

Take a short walk from the main square to the *Villa Cimbrone* on *Via Santa Chiara, 26.* The belvedere gives superb views.

The church of *San Giovanni del Torro* is well worth a visit. There's much of interest inside.

This brief description scarcely begins to describe the delights of Ravello. For more information you really should visit www.ravello.com. It's very informative, and click on Ravello Virtual Tour for a display of superb photographs that really show the delights that this area has to offer.

Rome

The ultimate day trip, although some stay overnight or for the weekend. It's 240km from Sorrento, a four hour drive, but can you be so near to the Eternal City and not pay it a visit? On the other hand there's so much to see in Rome that you can't do it in either one or two days, and it's a long journey. You can rocket around the sites, but it won't do any of them justice. Spare yourself the exhaustion of a whirlwind visit and see Rome in its own right sometime. A week is not enough, but it's a whole lot better than a couple of days.

The usual big city warning - watch out for beggars and pickpockets. The most common beggars are women of swarthy appearance, frequently carrying a baby. Say "No" emphatically and walk away from them.

My own close encounter with a pickpocket was on a bus, crowded as usual. I suddenly realized that a hand was in my pocket. I was wearing outdoor trousers with a double zip pocket. He had already got past one zip. I scrunched his fingers together and yelled at him. No one else on the bus paid any attention. If we hadn't been so closely packed together I might have felt compelled to rearrange his features, especially as he was smaller than me. He got off at the next stop. He looked every inch a businessman. He had a briefcase tucked under his arm. He never once looked at me. I was pleased to see that he looked pained. He stood in the queue, waiting for the next bus. So you can't tell by appearances.

Now to more pleasant things. Rome is just one vast, outdoor museum. Everywhere you go there seems to be another masterpiece of some sort, even with the pavement artists. The usual sights that you will read about in any guide include:

St Peters

This is a must. It would be a pity not to be allowed in because you are not wearing acceptable clothing.

The sheer size of the place is almost unimaginable. No matter how many times you've seen it on television, you won't believe how vast St Peters is, both the square and the building itself.

Inside St Peters is unforgettable. I don't have the words to describe it adequately You can take a lift or steps up to a roof level and look down on the square. From there you can go inside to get to the very top of St Peters. It uses a one way system inside. This means that when you emerge onto the roof top area again, it's a different area from the one you left from.

When I went with my wife, she didn't fancy the climb to the top and waited for me. It was a long time after I came out of the building again before I realized that she was somewhere else. Going wrong way back through the one way system can meet with some very non-Christian looks!

Before our holiday I had done my usual brush up of the language and decided that I was going to make more use of it. The flaw soon appeared. I found that while I could ask questions, I usually couldn't understand the answers. But I tried. Wanting to know the way to the Sistine Chapel

I approached one official. I'd revised it before, so I confidently said,

"Mi scusi. Dov'è la Capella Sistina per favore?"

"It's round there on the left," he said.

I might as well have had a Union Jack tattooed on my forehead.

Trevi Fountain

The fountain is hidden down what would just about rate as a back street, but turn the corner and the sight will take your breath away. Again it's beyond anything you may have imagined. Maybe Anita Ekberg managed to look decorative in it, in Fellini's *La Dolce Vita*, but anyone encroaching on it now is stopped immediately - not by the *Carabinieri*, who are too busy posing in their magnificent uniforms, but by the local police whistle, and people tend not to argue with them.

There's a tradition of throwing coins into the fountain, but not just any way. You should stand with your back to the fountain, hold the coin in your right hand and throw it over your left shoulder. Throwing a coin into the Trevi ensures that one day you will return to Rome.

You need to be watchful while all this coin throwing is going on. One person I know of was the happy recipient of a coin in his ear. He's probably now being stalked by someone who has a strange, compelling urge to find him again.

Spanish Steps

A seating and meeting point for the local youth, for backpackers, and for those who are too hot to make it all the way to the top without stopping for a breather. It marks one end of the *Via Condotti*, where you can spend all your worldly wealth in no time at all in the big name fashion houses. If you are in a rush and have invested most of your euros in the shops, you can grab a quick snack in the nearby McDonalds.

Pantheon

The Pantheon is on *Piazza della Rotonda*.

If you've read Dan Brown's "Angels & Demons" you will have come across the Pantheon. It's a round building illuminated by light coming through the oculus, a circular opening in the vast dome. This light can make for some interesting photos.

The Pantheon was built by the Emperor Hadrian in the first century AD. It's rather like a dome built on top of a cylinder. The radius of the dome is equal to the height of the cylinder, so its proportions are beautifully symmetrical.

Piazza Navona

This is another lovely area. It's just a short walk from the Pantheon. It used to be the site of Roman chariot races; hence the oval shape. Now it's a site for artists who add colour to the area. It's very pleasant to sit here and watch the world go by.

There are three fountains, the most famous being the Fountain of the Four Rivers (*Fontana dei Quattro Fiumi*) by Gian Lorenzo Bernini. Figures symbolise the rivers Nile, Plate, Danube and Ganges.

The other two fountains were both created by Giacomo Della Porta. They are the Fountain of Neptune (*Fontana del Nettuno*) and the Moor fountain (*Fontana del Moro*).

A walk to the Colosseum

A good starting point for a walk to the Colosseum is from the *Piazza Venezia*, dominated by the monument to King Victor Emmanual II. It's an interesting challenge to consider how you could cross the piazza on foot as the traffic whizzes around.

When I was last there, a wedding car with bride and groom waving to the world at large, and followed by two other cars, presumably from the same wedding party, made many circuits with horns blaring, responded to by every other car in the area with a toot of its own horn. It was bedlam, but this is Italy.

On the way you pass the Forum. As we stood and wondered about its place in Roman history and the stories it could tell, an American voice close to us, speaking to her companion, said "You'd think they'd keep it in a better state of repair". OK, it has seen better days, but it would lose something in the process.

The Colosseum symbolises Rome. It dates from AD72. It was built by Emperor Vespasian. It held up to 55,000 spectators to witness the bloodthirsty spectacles. Think what it was like in the days of the gladiators. Practice your own gladiatorial skills fending off the freelance tourist guides. Feed the cats. Nobody much else does.

Salerno

Salerno is the second city of Campania.

Excursions to Salerno are twinned with Paestum. Salerno is a city and a major port, some 50km from Sorrento. Attractions are the cathedral, other churches, and the shops.

The allied troops landed here during the Second World War.

Solfatara

Usually combined with a visit to nearby Naples, it is the site of a dormant volcano. It is a part of the Phlegraean Fields, the area around Pozzuoli which is still subject to volcanic activity. If you've survived Naples, now you can live dangerously here.

Vesuvius (Vesuvio)

Background

The height of Vesuvius is currently 1281m. It changes with each eruption. Go now before it gets any higher.

You've heard of two for the price of one? Well here you've got a volcano within a volcano. At one time there was only Mount Somma. Vesuvius was formed when Mount Somma collapsed, and now sits within the crater that was then formed. This was about 15,000 years ago. Vesuvius is the only live volcano on the mainland of Europe. Its name comes from the Greek word for fire.

The eruption that covered Pompeii, Herculaneum and Stabia was preceded by a series of tremors. Then on 24th August in AD79, just before midday, there was a powerful earthquake. This was followed an hour or so later by the eruption, sending a cloud of ash and dust up into the air. What goes up must come down, and so it did, onto the surrounding countryside, with devastating effect.

Volcanologists say that another major eruption is long overdue. Several years ago one expert put the odds at 50% for an eruption in the following year. The odds must inevitably shorten with every passing year, but 50% did seem a bit high.

Half a million people live within a four-mile radius of the volcano, and up to three million people would face evacuation in the event of a major eruption. Some estimates put the possible death toll at up to 300,000, and if you have seen Italian drivers you can assume that most of these would be road accidents as they fled the area.

What happened in AD79?

I wish I could tell you. I haven't got a definitive answer. After researching various sources, it seems that:

- All that everyone agrees on is that it happened on 24 August in AD79, and was preceded by a powerful earthquake.

- Some say Herculaneum was destroyed first. Others that it was Pompeii. Maybe the difference was whether they were talking about who experienced the first stuff falling from the sky or which population was totally annihilated first.

- A cloud of ash, rocks, pumice and gas were fired up to a height of 14km or maybe it was 32km.

- There have been 36 eruptions since then. Or was it more than 50?

- The temperature of the pyroclastic flow was 700C. Or 500C. Or 300C. Whichever, it was pretty warm.

- The pyroclastic flow travelled at 100mph or 80mph.

In case the volcanic terminology is confusing, magma is molten rock, lava is magma that is flowing from a volcano, and a pyroclastic flow is what would have been lava except that it has been superheated, fired up into the air, collapsed down again and is whizzing down the volcano side at a speed much faster than you can run. Experts reading this would probably want to qualify it all in a way that would fill many more inches and would make your eyes glaze over. Let's just settle for it being an environment that would make you wish you had gone to Bognor Regis instead.

Getting there

If you go on one of the excursions you will probably have

about 90 minutes there. This is enough time to get up to the crater and back, but does limit the time that you can spend at the top.

If you want more time you could try a taxi. If you do this, take the train to Ercolano and pick up a cab there. Negotiate a fee. Ensure that it's for the cab and not per person, that it's for the return journey, and that the driver will wait for you. Agree how long he is willing to wait. Carry paper and pen, and ask him to write down the agreed fare. And don't pay until you are back to the starting point.

From the railway station at Ercolano you can also take a local bus, but check the times. It's a long walk back if you miss the last one. It's best to check the times via a timetable, and not by what loitering private bus and taxi drivers might say. They could have ulterior motives.

Your transport will have taken you most of the way up the crater - to around 1000m or 3300 feet. The final 300m or 900 feet is on foot.

Ideal footwear would be walking boots. Trainers are OK, but will never look quite the same again, so if they cost a fortune and are your pride and joy, you need to bear this in mind. Open toed sandals and high heels are a definite no-no, even though this seems to be the footwear of choice for some who have not been adequately warned.

As you approach the entrance you will find toilets are on your left, behind some panelling. There is a voluntary charge of 50c that no one seems to pay. They are a bit grim.

The standard entry fee is €10.00. Try to give the exact

money as they are said to have problems with change.

Going Up

A funicular to the summit opened in 1880 amid much rejoicing and inspired the song *Funiculì-Funiculà*. It was badly damaged in the eruption of 1906. It was repaired but the upper station was then damaged by a further eruption in 1911. It survived the 1929 eruption, but finally succumbed in 1944 to the last eruption. Work started on a new funicular in 1991, but was later abandoned. A chairlift operated from 1953 to 1984. Now there is no alternative to get to the top other than on foot.

The walk is over loose volcanic gravel and stones. You will be offered sticks to aid your walk at the start. These are free. But some recompense, around one or two euros, is expected when you return the sticks, and the attendants will be greatly disappointed if you forget to provide this. A disappointed Italian is a sight to behold. A stick is undeniably helpful, two sticks more so, but if you are carrying much gear, e.g. cameras, water, small children, you may not have enough hands to cope.

It's unlikely that you will be able to get to the furthest stretches around the rim of the crater in the time allowed on organised excursions. The rim of the crater is about 1.6km around its perimeter. This is too far to allow you to do a full circuit in the time that you will be allowed. You will need to allow at least 40 minutes for the ascent and descent. You will probably also want to spend some time looking down into the crater, back at Naples, and taking photographs and videos.

Time yourself on the journey up, and assume that it will take as long to go down again. This will let you know how long you've got before returning. Not quite true of course. It's faster going down, but it will mean that you are not last onto the coach and suffering the glares of those already on board.

In the summer of 1980 I made my first trip to the top. It was possible then to go down a little way into the crater with a guide. There were some signs of volcanic activity then, with steam or smoke hissing out of fissures (*fumaroles*), but in 2007 on my last ascent it seemed to be totally dead and was pretty much how I envisage the surface of the moon, so no plumes of smoke or bubbling cauldron of lava. Hope this isn't a disappointment after your exertions.

You can't now descend into the crater: it's fenced off. This is not a major obstacle to idiots, but just don't do it. The depth of the crater from the rim is 300m, so you don't want to fall over the edge.

Will it blow again?

The monitoring of the volcano is done constantly. According to a tour guide, the observatory, equipped with a formidable array of equipment, will be able to give eight days warning of an impending eruption. Other information imparted by this guide was a bit questionable, so maybe realistic forecasting is a little more short term than that.

If you happen to see people running out of the observatory, screaming, it's perhaps time to consider the fastest way round to the other side of the bay.

What would it look like?

An eruption such as that in AD79 is known as Plinian, and tends to be in three phases: an explosion; a quiet phase; then the fireworks - ash, rocks, lapilli (small stones), toxic gas, lava. As a pyroclastic flow is both hot and fast you don't want to be around for this.

The name Plinian comes from Pliny the Younger, who gave the first eye witness account of the volcanic eruption in 79AD. His uncle, Pliny the Elder, was at the time in command of one of the Roman navies. He set out on a rescue mission, but treated it too casually. An unwise decision as it turned out. He didn't survive it. You can read the account at

http://www.eyewitnesstohistory.com/pompeii.htm

The eruption of Mount St Helens in Washington on May 18 1980 followed this pattern, except that it erupted sideways.

PART 4 HOTELS

GENERAL

There are said to be around 100 hotels in the Sorrento area. There are more than 50 hotels that I am aware of that are within about a 15 minute walk of the town centre. Those in Sant'Agnello are within reach of the Sorrento centre, but it can be a longish walk on a hot day. But there's always the buses or train. Hotels that are a little farther afield often run their own shuttle service into the centre. Taxis can be expensive. A ten minute ride can set you back €20 or more. The moral is not to miss the shuttle.

Most of the hotels that follow are ones that I have personally visited or stayed in. Some details are from reports sent to me by people who have bought the guide and have written about their experiences. Most of the hotels have sea views, some being on the cliffs, others being across the road, but with views from the higher floors. There are many other fine hotels. This is just a small sample.

Going around the hotels was an illuminating experience. I approached them all as a possible future guest. I wonder why more places, businesses as well as hotels, don't realise that reception is the first point of contact for many people. First impressions count for so much, and convey the attitude of the establishment. I had genuinely friendly greetings at two of the hotels. Most of the others I would regard as efficient rather than friendly.

If you want a quiet life, try for a hotel with rooms overlooking gardens, or sea views with no road intervening.

HOTELS

To The East Of Piazza Tasso

In order of increasing distances from Piazza Tasso are:

Hotel Carlton International

This is a modern hotel, just round the corner and about a couple of minutes' walk away from the Piazza Tasso. I have stayed there three times. It's a nice, light, airy, pleasant hotel. There is a sea view from the higher floors. There is a good pool and a nice area around it with free deck chairs. Sun loungers are chargeable.

Via Correale, 15 - 80067 - Sorrento, Italia

Phone: + 39 081 807 2669

Fax: + 39 081807 1073

E-mail: info@hotelcarltonsorrento.com

Web: www.hotelcarltonsorrento.com

Reservations: reservations@hotelcarltonsorrento.com

Hotel Eden

The Eden is next door to the Carlton, but set back more from the road.

Several years ago I had an unfortunate experience at the Eden - I stayed there. But it was several years ago. Hopefully, things will have changed for the better. I was on the first floor. It had no view of the sea from there. Higher floors may get a view of the sea. People I spoke to in July 2007 said that it was basic, but that the staff was friendly.

A couple staying there in 2012 were very happy with it, particularly the location with a back entrance onto *Corso Italia*. They thought their room was excellent. Later another couple didn't have much good to say about it. It seems that experience there can be highly variable.

Certainly the website now shows accommodation that is much better than I remember it.

Via Correale , 25 - 80067 - Sorrento, Italia

Phone: +39 081 878 1901

Fax: +39 081 807 2016

Web: http://www.hoteledensorrento.com/

Grand Hotel Europa Palace

This is a fine hotel looking out over the Bay. The girl on reception was most helpful, friendly and welcoming, and gave a very good impression. The Europa is across the road from Piazza Lauro, which makes it convenient for trains, tour buses, post office and banks, and is about a five minute walk to Piazza Tasso.

Via Correale, 34/36 - 80067 – Sorrento, Italia

Phone :   +39 081 807 3432

Fax: +39 081 807 4384

E-mail: info@europapalace.com

Web:
          http://www.europapalace.com/en/index.php

Reservations: reservation@europapalace.com

Grand Hotel Royal

The Royal is next door to the Europa with the same convenience and views across the Bay.

Via Correale, 42 – PO BOX 83 - 80067 - Sorrento - Italia

Phone: +39 081 8073434

Fax: +39 081 8772905

Email: info@manniellohotels.com

Web:https://www.royalsorrento.com:441/en/index.php

Grand Hotel Ambasciatori

The Ambasciatori is a little further from PiazzaTasso. It is also on the cliff top.

Via Califano, 18 - P.O. Box 101 - 80067 – Sorrento, Italia

Phone: +39 081 878 2025

Fax: +39 081 807 1021

Email: ambasciatori@manniellohotels.com

Web: http://www.ambasciatorisorrento.com

Grand Hotel Riviera

The Riviera stands in its own grounds, again on the cliff top, and is the furthest of these hotels from Piazza Tasso - about 15 minutes.

Via Aniello Califano, 22 - 80067 – Sorrento, Italia

Phone: +39 081 807 2011

Fax: +39 081 877 2100

Email: info@hotelriviera.com

Web: http://www.hotelriviera.com/en/

In Piazza Tasso

Grand Hotel Excelsior Vittoria.

The Excelsior is in the prime location in Sorrento. The entrance is in the Piazza, but the drive is so long that it will take about a couple of minutes to get from hotel to Piazza. This is another cliff top location.

There is normally an attendant on duty at the entrance to interrogate unsavoury characters like me, who attempt to gain admission. Having breached the outer defences and made it to the hotel, I then had the distinct impression that I was lowering the tone of the place in my outdoor gear. See my earlier comments on reception staff. It means that although I may one day stay here, if only so I don't have to sneak past the sentry on the gate, it's not the next one on my list. As befits a hotel that has been graced by people like Caruso, it is a class joint, with very extensive grounds.

Piazza Tasso, 34 - 80067 – Sorrento, Italia

Phone: +39 081 877 71 11

Fax: +39 081 877 1206

Email: info@exvitt.it

Web: www.exvitt.it/

Reservations: reservation@exvitt.it

On Corso Italia

The Corso Italia is a very busy road, so bear in mind that if you have a room facing the road, you are likely to notice the traffic.

Hotel Michelangelo

The Michelangelo is a very fine looking hotel on the Corso Italia a little to the east of Piazza Lauro. It's only a couple of minutes from a supermarket, and maybe 7 or 8 minutes' walk to Piazza Tasso in the centre of Sorrento. Being close to Piazza Lauro means that it is handily placed for banks, post office, excursion buses and the railway station, so you are very handily placed for whatever you want to do.

It is set a little way back from the road, which is just as well because it is a busy road. All the rooms are sound proofed.

Via Corso Italia 275 – 80067 – Sorrento, Italia

Phone :   +39 081 878 4844

Fax: +39 081 878 1816

Email: info@michelangelohotel.it

Web: http://www.michelangelohotel.it/

Hotel del Corso

The Corso is only a couple of minutes to the west of Piazza Tasso but is right on the road. It's on the second floor of an 18th century building. You can look down on the *passeggiata*.

Corso Italia, 134 - 80067 - Sorrento, Italia

Phone: +39 081 807 1016

Fax: +39 081 807 3157

Email: info@hoteldelcorso.com

Web: http://www.hoteldelcorso.com/

Hotel Plaza

This hotel is on a road leading out of *Piazza Tasso* and just three or four minutes' walk away.

I received two glowing reports from people who had enjoyed their time there.

Via Fuorimura, 3 - 80067 - Sorrento, Italia

Phone: +39 081 878 2831

Fax: +39 081 807 3942

Email: info@plazasorrento.com

Web: http://www.plazasorrento.com/en/

Three hotels at the west end of the Corso, about a ten minute walk from Piazza Tasso are:

Hotel Tirrenia

It's on the bay side of the road, but has traffic on both sides. It's the first hotel you come to after passing the hospital.

Via Capo, n.2- 80067 - Sorrento Italia

Phone :   +39 081 878 1336

Email: info@hoteltirrenia.com

Web:
        http://www.hoteltirrenia.com/main.php?LinguaN ew=Inglese

Hotel Rivage

Also on the bay side of the road

Via Capo, 11 - 80067- Sorrento, Italia

Phone: +39 081 878 1873

Fax: +39 081 807 1253

Web: http://www.hotelrivage.com/

Hotel Ascot

Across the road. It seems a bit Spartan and reports are not really glowing.

Via Capo, 6 - 80067 - Sorrento, Italia

Phone: +39 081 878 3032

Fax: +39 081 807   3013

Email: info@hotelascotsorrento.com

Web: http://www.hotelascotsorrento.com/

At Marina Piccola

There is only one hotel at this Marina:

Hotel Il Faro

This hotel is right at the Marina. A friend who stayed there some years ago was happy with it, and it's certainly handy for the boats, although it's quite a stiff climb up to the town. About six minutes will see you to the foot of the steps up to Piazza Tasso. Then there are the 130 steps up. Think how fit you will be at the end of the holiday if you do this trip twice a day for a fortnight. I did it just once, some years ago, and I've nearly got over it now.

Via Marina Piccola, 5- 80067 – Sorrento, Italia

Phone: +39 081 878 1390

Fax: +39 081 807 3144

Email: info@hotelifaro.com

Web: http://www.hotelilfaro.com/en.html

Around Piazza della Vittoria

This is a fine location for hotels. It's right on the edge of the old town. Just a couple of minutes or so and you'll be at Davide's Gelateria, A ten minute walk will take you to Piazza Tasso. Ten minutes along Via Marina Grande will lead to the fishermen's port. What's not to like about this area?

Imperial Hotel Tramontano

I have stayed at the Tramontano. It is built into the cliff side, with sea views from bedrooms and dining room. I was in a room that had a huge balcony on the face of the cliff. Sitting there in the evening, under the stars, listening to a tenor somewhere along the Bay singing Caruso was an unforgettable experience.

There often seems to be something happening here. The Head of State called on a visit to Sorrento. A fashion show was held while I was there.

It has nice grounds and an impressive foyer.

Via Vittorio Veneto, 1 - 80067 - Sorrento, Italia

Phone: +39 081 878 25 88

Fax: +39 081 807 2344

Email: info@hoteltramontano.it

Web: http://www.hoteltramontano.com/

Hotel Bellevue Syrene

Also on the cliff top, and with a sensational entrance. I've got this one marked down for my next visit. It's an easy stroll to just about anywhere from here. The views are as spectacular as the approach.

Piazza della Vittoria, 5 - 80067 - Sorrento Italia

Phone: +39 081 878 1024

Fax: +39 081 878 3963

Email: info@bellevue.it

Web: http://www.bellevue.it/

Hotel Continental

I've stayed here, too. It's a lovely hotel, just over the road from the cliff edge and with sea views. Some of the rooms have a side sea view and look down on the Grand Piazza della Vittoria, which was a haven of peace and quiet on a previous visit, but became the meeting place for the youth of the area on their scooters when I stayed there. But this only seemed to happen on that one occasion. Since then it's resumed its air of tranquillity whenever I have been in the area.

Piazza della Vittoria, 4 - 80067 – Sorrento, Italia

Phone: +39 081 8072608

Fax: +39 081 8782255

Email: info@continentalsorrento.com

Web: http://www.continentalsorrento.com/

Hotel Regina

Actually the Regina is about a couple of hundred metres beyond the Piazza and is just over the road from the Villa Pompeiana, which is a restaurant attached to the Hotel Bellevue Syrene.

Rooms at the front of the hotel will have sea views. It has free WiFi.

Via Marina Grande, 10 - 80067 - Sorrento, Italia

Phone: +39 081 878 2162

Fax: +39 081 8088 050

Email: info@hotelreginasorrento.com

Web: http://www.hotelreginasorrento.com/en

At Marina Grande

Hotel Admiral

It would be impossible to get nearer to the water than this. Last time I was there, a girl was sea fishing from the patio area which is built out over the water.

Being at the Marina, it has easy access to the sea front cafes and bathing beaches, but is a bit of a hike to the rest of the resort, probably about 25 minutes or so to Tasso, although I've never timed it.

Via Marina Grande, 214 - 80067 - Sorrento

Phone: +39 081 878 1076

Fax: +39 081 807 1076

Email: info@admiralsorrento.com

Web: http://www.gigliohotels.com/admiral

On The Road West Out Of Sorrento

At the end of the shopping area of Sorrento the Corso
Italia ends. It has come quite a distance to this point - all
the way from Vico Equense. It now becomes Via Capo, and
all the following hotels are on Via Capo.

The consideration for these hotels is that they are all on a
busy road. There is a footpath on only one side. It is very
narrow in places, and near the Tonnarella in one place it
would be difficult to find room for a pushchair. Beyond
the Tonnarella, the footpath peters out altogether. Going
into town is all downhill. This means, of course, that it's
all uphill on the way back, and this is a consideration if
you are hot and tired. And remember the proximity of
Italian drivers, not noted for regarding pedestrians as
anything other than expendable. That is the downside.
The upside is that the views are possibly the finest in
Sorrento, and there are some excellent hotels. They look
down over Marina Grande, and by the time you get to the
Tonnarella you can see both Marinas.

Also, during the various festivities, of which there seem to be many, and particularly at the end of the Festival of Sant Anna, the firework display is right in front of you.

In order, at increasing distances from the edge of the town are:

Grand Hotel Capodimonte

The website suggests that it is in Sorrento centre, but in fact it is an eight minute walk up from the Cathedral. Still, that's not far. It's set in the hillside. You therefore have to cross the road to reach the sanctuary of the pavement, which is wide enough at this point to take three people abreast.

It's a fine hotel with excellent facilities, and is highly regarded. It has five pools! Their layout is mind boggling.

Rooms on the lower floors don't have sea views, so if this is important to you, then check before booking. There are superb views from higher floors.

Reception is on the 5th Floor. I spoke to a couple in the lift as I made my way up to reception. They said it was the best hotel they had ever been to. They came last year too.

Via Capodimonte, 16/18 - 80067 - Sorrento, Italia

Phone: +39 081 878 4555

Fax: +39 081 807 1193

Email: capodimonte@manniellohotels.com

Web: www.capodimontesorrento.com/

Hotel Bristol

Another four minutes up the road from the Capodimonte and you come to the Bristol.

I visited friends while they were staying there. They were very happy with it, and I was impressed with what I saw. Most rooms have sea views, but you will have to check. The swimming pool is on the roof of the hotel. The view is stunning from there. It also has a gym where you can work off your holiday excesses.

Reviews of this hotel are among the best in the resort. Again you have to cross the road to reach the pavement.

Via Capo, 22 - 80067 - Sorrento, Italia

Phone: +39 081 878 4522

Fax: +39 081 807 1910

Email: bristol@acampora.it

Web:
              http://www.bristolsorrento.com/en/index.php

Hotel Minerva

Another hotel on the wrong side of the road, but with views from the dining room and rooftop swimming pool that are out of this world.

Via Capo, 30 - 80067 – Sorrento, Italia

Phone: +39 081 878 1011

Fax: +39 081 878 1949

Email: minerva@acampora.it

Web: http://www.minervasorrento.com/

This web page is in Italian, so you may have to translate it

Hotel Settimo Cielo

This hotel had the friendliest reception of them all and made me feel most welcome. It is on the sea side of the road and, according to the brochure, so are all the rooms.

Via Capo, 27 - 80067 - Sorrento, Italia

Phone: +39 081 878 1012

Fax: +39 081.8073290

Email: info@hotelsettimocielo.com

Web: http://www.hotelsettimocielo.com/

The web page is in Italian

Hotel Belair

On the sea side again. All rooms are said to have a sea view.

Via Capo, 29 - 80067 - Sorrento, Italia

Phone: +39 081 807 1622

Fax: +39 081 807 1467

E-mail: info@belair.it

Web: http://www.belair.it/en/

La Tonnarella

Beyond this hotel the pavement ceases to exist, but it's not quite the end of civilisation as we know it. There are more hotels beyond here, but I set my limit at about 15 minutes from the centre, and the Tonnarella itself is a little beyond that. From here to the edge of the shopping area is about 12 minutes. The Tonnarella has a lift down to its own beach.

Via Capo, 31 - 80067 - Sorrento, Italia

Phone: +39 081 878 1153

Fax.:   +39 081 878 2169

Email: info@latonnarella.it

Web: http://www.latonnarella.com/en/

AND FINALLY

I've taken every care in writing this guide, but mistakes happen, and I'm as prone to them as anyone else.

I hope that you find it useful during your time in Sorrento. You may have needed information that I haven't provided. If so, please let me know. I would especially appreciate it if you have also found the answers.

When you return I would love to hear of your experiences and any updates that you may have noticed. My email address is:

gordon@sorrentoguide.com.

I'd also really appreciate it if you could take a moment to leave a review of the guide, either after you've had the time to read it, or after your stay in Sorrento when you may have been able to put it to use.

Finally, thank you for buying the guide. If it has done anything to add to your enjoyment of this beautiful area, then it will have served its purpose.

Maybe one day you, too, will come back to Sorrento.

Gordon Longworth

July 2016

28594434R00081

Printed in Great Britain
by Amazon